WATERSHED Investigations

12 Labs for High School Science

WATERSHED Investigations

12 Labs for High School Science

Jennifer Soukhome, Graham Peaslee, Carl Van Faasen, and William Statema

NSTA press
National Science Teachers Association
Arlington, Virginia

National Science Teachers Association

Claire Reinburg, Director

Jennifer Horak, Managing Editor

Judy Cusick, Senior Editor

Andrew Cocke, Associate Editor

Art and Design
Will Thomas, Jr., Director—Cover and Interior Design

Printing and Production
Catherine Lorrain, Director

Nguyet Tran, Assistant Production Manager

National Science Teachers Association
Francis Q. Eberle, PhD, Executive Director

David Beacom, Publisher

11 10 09 4 3 2 1

Library of Congress Cataloging-in-Publication Data
Watershed investigations: 12 labs for high school science / by Jennifer Soukhome ... [et al.].

p. cm.

ISBN 978-1-933531-48-9

1. Watersheds—Study and teaching (Secondary)—Activity programs. 2. Watershed ecology—Study and teaching (Secondary)—Activity programs. 3. Water quality—Study and teaching (Secondary)—Activity programs. 4. Watershed hydrology—Study and teaching (Secondary)—Activity programs. 5. Stream measurements—Study and teaching (Secondary)—Activity programs. I. Soukhome, Jennifer.

GB1002.25.W38 2009

551.48078—dc22

2009011292

NSTA is committed to publishing material that promotes the best in inquiry-based science education. However, conditions of actual use may vary, and the safety procedures and practices described in this book are intended to serve only as a guide. Additional precautionary measures may be required. NSTA and the authors do not warrant or represent that the procedures and practices in this book meet any safety code or standard of federal, state, or local regulations. NSTA and the authors disclaim any liability for personal injury or damage to property arising out of or relating to the use of this book, including any of the recommendations, instructions, or materials contained therein.

CONTENTS

CONTENTS

PREFACE

This lab manual was developed over the past three summers as a result of our efforts to study the environmental anthropogenic effects on watersheds. Most of the labs examine the ecological consequences that can happen in a watershed as urbanization increases and natural hydrology changes, while some of the labs have been included to provide necessary background information that is needed before completing later investigations.

The premise of this lab manual is that it can be used in any high school experiment-based environmental science curriculum. This manual is appropriate for upper high school students, as well as the younger grades. For example, modified laboratory procedures for this manual have been tested in a 9th grade Earth science classroom. By the nature of environmental science, the experiments cover a broad range of disciplines: geology, chemistry, Earth science, and biology and meet a wide array of state and national curricular standards. Each laboratory contains ideas to suggest in what type of class the teacher may find the laboratory useful.

There are 12 different laboratory exercises included and half of them have an extensive open-ended inquiry approach that we feel is essential for conveying some of the excitement of discovery along with the methods of scientific research and relevant examples of textbook subject material. Each laboratory could be taught in a traditional prescriptive manner, but we encourage the high school teacher to adopt some of or all of the inquiry-based learning activities included in many of the laboratories. As an example the "Allelopathy" investigation in Chapter 5 has students compare invasive and/or native plants and how their chemical components may affect the germination rate of lettuce seeds. The students develop a hypothesis and design an experiment to test the problem. They are given the methods by which to extract the chemicals from the plant material and tools for statistical testing. In another investigation, students compare the effect of stream channel morphology on the rate of sediment transport by using a Styrofoam stream table. As in the allelopathy lab, students must develop a hypothesis and design an experiment to test it.

PREFACE

When students in our classes are first asked to do a lab as inquiry, quite a bit of resistance is typically encountered. For most students, this will be the first opportunity for them to develop an investigation in a science class. A lot of time needs to be spent reassuring the students and repeating the steps of development and referring them back to their instruction sheet. However, after the first inquiry lab or two, future inquiry labs will be a lot less demanding on the teacher as students will be familiar with the expectations. After a term with many inquiry labs, many students are enthusiastic for more.

When conducting inquiry labs with students, it is always fascinating to see what the students develop and in what direction they take the lab. Instead of having the same lab that all students complete, the result is a variety of different lab procedures which all have been designed to examine the same problem. Since the students are responsible for the development of the lab, form their own hypothesis, and analyze their own data, they seem to have better retention of the information. Teachers can often learn from the students' results and students will teach each other in many cases.

Another advantage of having several different labs is that while there always is a chance of lab failure when there are several different labs being conducted the chances are that most of them will convey what was desired. In addition, the teacher is there guiding the students through the process, giving approval to their procedures and learning from the results just as the students do. This can often transform the teacher from a central authority figure to a coach on a shared adventure. Classroom discussion of everyone's lab about what worked and what didn't is always recommended. It does give students a chance to see that science is a process and sometime things may not work as planned. On the flip side, your students may discover new things that you had not thought of and bring in a new perspective as ours have done in almost every inquiry-based lab.

It is hard to turn over the control of your classroom to the students and give them some autonomy, but it is well worth it. Since we have been using inquiry labs and field work, we have seen students become more excited about their learning. We often have students tell us they shared what they learned with their friends or family. We have even had some students gain such an interest that they have decided to pursue a career in science. Here is an example of one such case. Stacy came into one of our classes as a senior and was decidedly going to school for culinary arts after graduation. Upon the completion of the course she wrote, "I would like to further my education in plants or animals and this hooked my interest in this type of study. I really did enjoy this class a lot."

Other labs in the manual emphasize field work and critical thinking skills. One of the field exercises teaches students how to identify plants. In a more traditional data analysis lab, students use data from the USGS website to construct a hydrograph of a river and predict the recurrence interval and probability of different flooding episodes. There is plenty of background information for teachers who may not be comfortable with these topics.

As you can see from the table below most of the labs cover the inquiry strand in the Michigan science curriculum and in the national standards.

Table 1. Michigan and National Science Standards Covered by Labs

Chapter in Lab Manual	Michigan Curriculum Objectives Covered	National Science Standards Covered
Ch 1: Modeling Glacial Features with Sand	E3.p1A E4.p3A	C.4.b.13
Ch 2: Glacial Features of a Watershed	E4.p3C	C.4.b.13
Ch 3: Plant Identification		C.2.a.2
Ch 4: Wetland Delineation	E4.p1D	C.2.b.20
Ch 5: Allelopathy	B1.1-ALL B1.2A-D B1.2f,j,k B3.4C B3.5C	C.2.a.2,3 C.2.b.14,20 C.2.c.25
Ch 6: Stream Channel Morphology	E1.1-ALL E1.2A-D E1.2f,j,k E3.p1B E4.p1C	C.4.a.3 C.4.b.19,21
Ch 7: Calculating Stream Discharge	E4.p1B	C.4.c.26
Ch 8: Flood Frequency Analysis	E4.p1C	C.4.c.26
Ch 9: Comparison of Phosphorus Levels in Stream Sediments	E1.1-ALL E1.2A-D E1.2f,j,k E4.1C	C.2.b.18,20
Ch 10: Aquatic Macroinvertebrates as Water Quality Indicators		C.4.a.12
Ch 11: Factors that Affect Eutrophication	E1.1-ALL E1.2A-D E1.2f,j,k E4.1C	C.2.b.18,20
Ch 12: Groundwater Contamination	E1.1-ALL E1.2A-D E1.2f,j,k E3.p1B E4.p1C	C.4.a.12 C.4.b.21

The labs in this manual are presented in a logical order although they do not need to be completed in this order. Furthermore, the teacher does not need to complete all of the labs and does not need to feel locked into any type of format. In certain instances the lab may fit into the class better as inquiry-based and at others only the traditional approach would work. A teacher that is not familiar with the material or inquiry learning may choose the traditional approach only for the first year until their comfort level increases. All of the investigations contain a large portion of background information whereas the student sheets contain the bare minimum, the teacher can cut and paste this background information as they see fit. Teachers should be able to use all these investigations right out of the book but also could choose to tailor any of the investigations to fit their own classroom needs.

While this laboratory manual was written with a specific watershed in mind, teachers all over the United States will be able to use the experiments. Reference information is given when appropriate for teachers to access information for their own watershed. However, teachers may wish to use the book as is and turn the watershed this book was based on into a case study for their classrooms. In that event, a brief history of the watershed has been included as an appendix at the back of this manual with a website where additional information can be obtained. In addition, teachers will also find a rubric for writing laboratory reports and the corresponding rubric in the appendix as well.

The experiments in this manual were developed, classroom tested, and written up as a result of a collaborative effort coordinated by Dr. Graham Peaslee, supported by Hope College, the National Science Foundation, the Michigan Space Grant Consortium, the Holland/Zeeland Community Foundation, and the Macatawa Coordinating Council. We would like to thank the following people in particular for their support: Dr. Winnett Murray, Dr. Cronkite, Dr. Murray, Dr. Stewart all from Hope College, Holland Michigan and Sue Higgins and Beth McDonald both from the Macatawa Area Coordinating Council, Holland, Michigan.

ABOUT THE AUTHORS

Jennifer Soukhome earned her Bachelor Degree in Education from Ferris State University in 1996 where she majored in biology and minored in general science. She then went on to earn her chemistry certification and Masters Degree in Education with an emphasis in Biology from Grand Valley State University in 2002. She has been a high school science teacher since 1997 in Zeeland, Michigan at Zeeland West High School. During that tenure, she has taught 9-12th graders subjects ranging from academic support, biology, chemistry for the community, chemistry, physical science, earth science and wetland ecology. She wrote the curriculum for the wetland ecology class as her master thesis project and was awarded the Macatawa Watershed Stakeholder of the year award for the development of the wetland ecology class which has been successfully running since 2003. Jennifer has been active in education during the summers by participating in Hope College's Howard Hughes Medical Institute Summer Research program where she has been a co-coordinator of the education scholars program for two summers. She resides in Holland, Michigan with her family.

Graham Peaslee is a professor of Chemistry and Environmental Science at Hope College, in Holland, Michigan. He received his bachelor's degree in chemistry from Princeton University, and his Ph.D. in chemical physics from SUNY Stony Brook. He is trained as a nuclear chemist and has been active in nuclear science research for more than 25 years. During this time he has published over 125 research articles. He has been at Hope College for the past 14 years and during that time has become heavily involved in undergraduate education and educational reform as well. He won the Hope Outstanding Professor and Educator award from the Hope College senior class of 2000, and has co-written several teaching cases, one on nuclear science published in the Journal of College Science Teaching. His research projects have expanded into environmental science, and he has helped to co-develop the environmental science minor at Hope College. He has been actively involved in the technical subcommittee of the Watershed Project of the Macatawa Area Coordinating Council and lives in the Macatawa Watershed with his family.

ABOUT THE AUTHORS

Carl Van Faasen was born and raised in Holland, Michigan. He graduated from Holland High School in 1987, and graduated with a B.S. from Hope College in 1992 where he majored in biology and chemistry and minored in physics and math. In 1999, he received his M.Ed from Grand Valley State University. He has been employed as a high school Chemistry teacher for the past 16 years, mostly at Holland High School. Currently he has been working to incorporate phosphorus monitoring in the curriculum by implementing a Macatawa Watershed class. He has a wife, Pamela, and two children, Neil and Cora.

William Statema was born in the small town of Zeeland, Michigan in 1984. He graduated from Zeeland High School in 2003, and earned his bachelor's degree in Chemistry Education from Hope College in 2007. After college, William moved out to the Chicagoland area where he is teaching chemistry in the Niles Township School District. William is happily married and continues to pursue further education in the sciences.

CHAPTER 1

Modeling Glacial Features With Sand

Teacher Information*

Background

There are two types of glaciers: *valley* and *continental.* Valley glaciers, also called alpine glaciers, exist in mountainous regions all over the world. Continental glaciers once covered one-third of North America during the Ice Age; today they exist in Greenland, Iceland, and Antarctica. All glaciers pick up rock and sediment, which is called plucking, as they flow across the earth. As they do this they leave erosional features called grooves and striations. Glaciers deposit the rock and sediment in two different ways. Some rock and sediment are directly deposited by the ice, and this is referred to as till. The most common form of till is the moraine, which is simply a hill of gravel with sand or clay. Depending on where the moraine is deposited in relation to the glacier, it is referred to as a lateral moraine or an end moraine. Rock and sediment that are deposited by the running water coming off the melting glacier are referred to as outwash. Examples of outwash features include outwash plains, kettle lakes, and eskers.

Valley glaciers have many erosional features that are easily recognized (see Figure 1.1). Before glaciation, mountain valleys have a characteristic V shape, produced by downward erosion by running water. During glaciation, these valleys widen and deepen, becoming more U-shaped. Cirques are bowl-shaped depressions found at the head of a valley glacier. When several cirques chisel a mountain from three or more sides, a pyramidal peak called a horn is formed. Arêtes are the narrow, serrated ridges that form when two cirques erode a mountain. Other features that are common from alpine glaciation include plucking, striations, grooves, end moraines, lateral moraines, outwash plains, and kettle lakes.

*This investigation was adapted from an article by Jacqueline Kane, "Geology on a sand budget," in *The Science Teacher* September 2004.

Figure 1.1. Erosional Features of Valley Glaciers

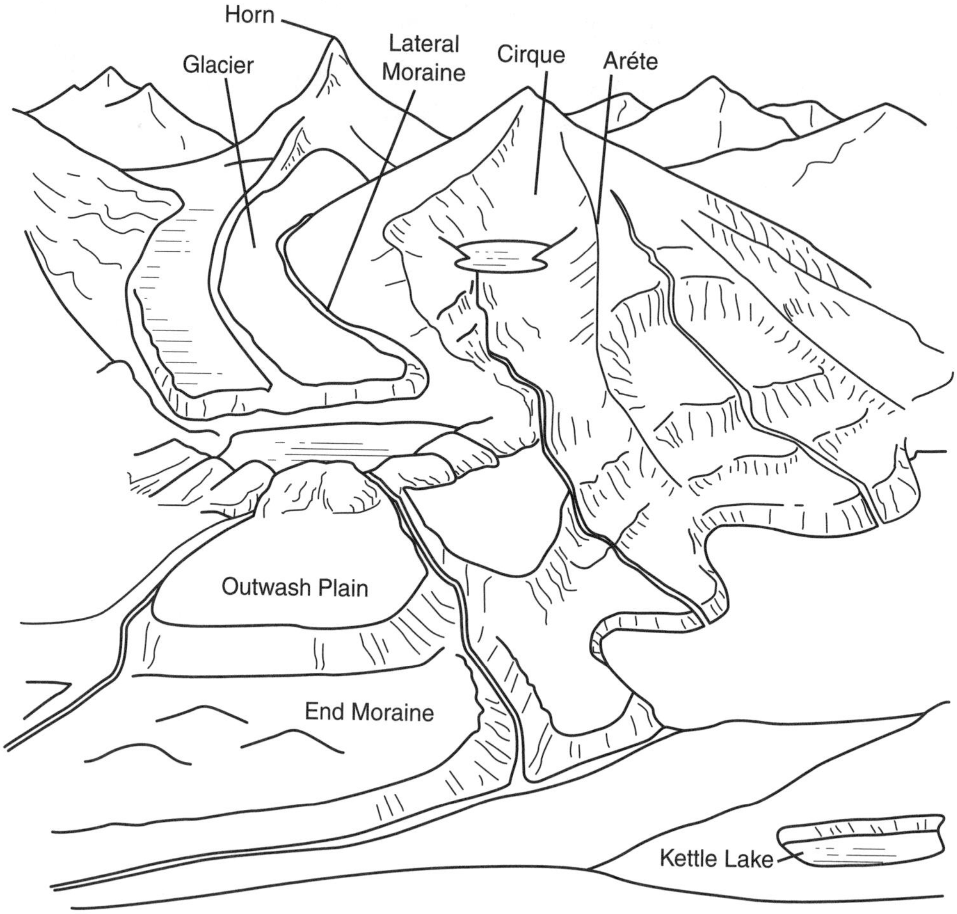

SCiLINKS
THE WORLD'S A CLICK AWAY
Topic: Glaciers
Go to: www.scilinks.org
Code: WAT001

Figure 1.2 illustrates the erosional features of continental glaciers. The continental glacier can deposit till in the forms of drumlins (egg-shaped moraines), end moraines, and lateral moraines. The melt water of the glacier makes deposits such as eskers, outwash plains, and kettle lakes. Plucking, grooves, and striations can also be seen when there is exposed bedrock (Pidwirny 2006).

Figure 1.2. Erosional Features of Continental Glaciers

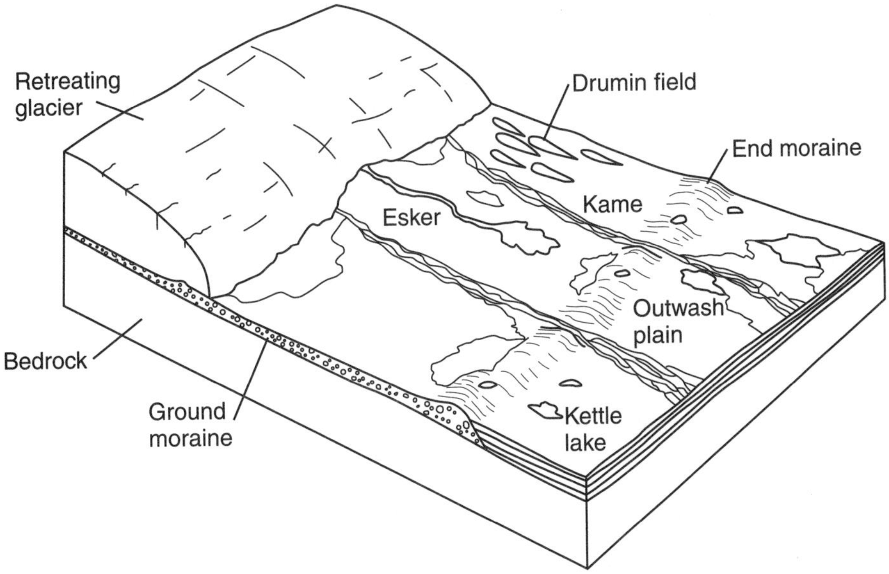

Objective

To make a model of the different erosional features of valley and continental glaciers out of sand and determine their impact on topography and hydrology.

Materials

- sand
- tubs/trays (shoe box size would work well)
- water
- plastic spoons
- laminated labels with glacial features taped to toothpicks

Suggested Class Preparation and Format

Some instruction about the different glacial features should take place before this investigation. The investigation would be best taught as part of a unit on glaciers and glaciation, but it could also be taught as part of a lesson on the topography of the northern United States. The investigation would also fit in nicely when teaching a unit on watersheds, to introduce the concept of how the topography of the land controls the hydrology, which in turn shapes the watershed.

Initial preparation involves the creation of laminated labels, which will take some time. Once these labels are made, preparation is minimal and the materials

SCILINKS
THE WORLD'S A CLICK AWAY

Topic: Glaciers, and Landforms
Go to: *www.scilinks.org*
Code: WAT002

can be reused every year. The investigation will take approximately 20 minutes for students to complete.

To prepare the labels, on a sheet of paper type up all of the terms students should be able to identify for both valley and continental glaciers, or use the checklist provided at the end of the Student Instructions section. Make enough copies for your students and have them laminated, then cut apart the terms and tape each one to a toothpick. Put each set of terms in a resealable bag. Make as many sets as necessary for your classroom. To save time, you can have students do some of this preparation.

As students model the glacial features, they should label them with the appropriate terms by inserting a toothpick with the appropriate label into each feature. Instruct students to raise their hands when features for each type of glacier are complete, so that you can check the labels for accuracy. Of course, when students finish at the same time some will have to wait. As an alternative to this teacher-centered model, you can create a grading rubric on paper and ask the students as they finish their own labels to begin to assess each other's landforms for accuracy. The grade sheets filled out by students can even be used as part of the formal assessment. In both cases it is also helpful to have the students bring in the handout with the checklist of erosional features, so they can check off the features they have made correctly. In addition, feel free to orally question the students about the features.

Student Procedure

1. Take one tub of sand, one bag of labels, and one spoon.
2. If your sand is not wet, add enough water to moisten the sand so it is the consistency to build sand castles with and not oversaturated.
3. Make a mountain range in your "sandbox" with all the erosional features associated with valley glaciers (refer to your features checklist).
4. Label the valley glacier features.
5. Raise your hand to have your teacher check your work before proceeding; after your teacher has checked your work, remove your labels.
6. Now make another mountain range in your sandbox with all the erosional features associated with continental glaciers.
7. Label the continental glacier features.
8. Again, raise your hand to have your teacher check your work; after your teacher has checked your work, remove your labels.

Checklist of Erosional Features of Valley (Alpine) and Continental Glaciers

- arête
- cirque
- drumlin
- end moraine
- esker
- grooves
- horn
- kettle lake
- lateral moraine
- outwash plain
- plucking
- striations
- U-shaped valley
- V-shaped valley

Answers to Questions in Student Handout

1. end moraine, lateral moraine, drumlin
2. esker, outwash plain, kettle lake
3. striations, grooves, plucking
4. horn, cirque, arête
5. Answers will vary depending on location; for example, students should say flat areas may be due to outwash features or hilly areas are from till deposits. Glaciers shaped the topography, which in turn determines the flow of water.

Reference

Pidwirny, M. 2006. Landforms of glaciation. In *Fundamentals of physical geography. 2nd ed.* *www.physicalgeography.net/fundamentals/10af.html*

Modeling Glacial Features With Sand

Student Handout

Background

There are two types of glaciers: *valley* and *continental.* Valley glaciers, also called alpine glaciers, exist in mountainous regions all over the world. Continental glaciers once covered one-third of North America during the Ice Age; today they exist in Greenland, Iceland, and Antarctica. All glaciers pick up rock and sediment, which is called plucking, as they flow across the earth. As they do this they leave erosional features called grooves and striations. Glaciers deposit the rock and sediment in two different ways. Some rock and sediment are directly deposited by the ice, and this is referred to as till. The most common form of till is the moraine, which is simply a hill of gravel with sand or clay. Depending on where the moraine is deposited in relation to the glacier, it is referred to as a lateral moraine or an end moraine. Rock and sediment that are deposited by the running water coming off the melting glacier are referred to as outwash. Examples of outwash features include outwash plains, kettle lakes, and eskers.

Objective

To make a model of the different erosional features of valley and continental glaciers out of sand and determine their impact on topography and hydrology.

Materials

- sand
- tubs/trays
- water
- plastic spoons
- laminated labels with glacial features taped to toothpicks

Procedure

1. Take one tub of sand, one bag of labels, and one spoon.
2. If your sand is not wet, add enough water to moisten the sand so it is the consistency to build sand castles with and not oversaturated.
3. Make a mountain range in your "sandbox" with all the erosional features associated with valley glaciers (refer to your features checklist). Not all items from the checklist will be used for the valley glacier.
4. Label the valley glacier features. You should have 12 features labeled.
5. Raise your hand to have your teacher check your work before proceeding; after your teacher has checked your work, remove your labels.
6. Now make another mountain range in your sandbox with all the erosional

features associated with continental glaciers.

7. Label the continental glacier features. You should have 9 features labeled. Some of the features will be the same ones you labeled on the valley glacier, and some will be different.
8. Again, raise your hand to have your teacher check your work; after your teacher has checked your work, remove your labels.

Checklist of Erosional Features of Valley (Alpine) and Continental Glaciers

- arête
- cirque
- drumlin
- end moraine
- esker
- grooves
- horn
- kettle lake
- lateral moraine
- outwash plain
- plucking
- striations
- U-shaped valley
- V-shaped valley

Name________________________________

Questions on Glacial Features

1. List all the glacial features on your list that are deposited from till.

2. List all the glacial features on your list that are deposited from outwash.

3. List the other glacial features not from till or outwash.

4. List all the features that are unique to valley glaciers.

5. Using what you learned from this lab activity, explain the effects of glaciers on topography and hydrology.

CHAPTER 2

Glacial Features of a Watershed

Teacher Information*

Background

About 9,000 years ago the last glacier to shape the topography of Michigan retreated from the Upper Peninsula. Because glacial drift covers most of Michigan, there are very few areas where bedrock is exposed. This is also true for most of the northern portion of the United States. As the glaciers advanced and retreated, they left sediments called glacial drift in two forms, referred to as till and outwash. Sediments deposited through till are called moraines and consist of piles (hills) of unsorted materials such as sand, mud, and gravel. Till was dumped by the glacier along its leading edge. As the glacier melted, the running water left flat plain areas called outwash plains. Sediments deposited through outwash are sorted by particle size, with the finer particles being transported the farthest.

The sediments deposited by the glacier through till and outwash shaped the topography of the northern United States. Michigan glaciations not only carved out the Great Lakes but also affect our lives today in other ways. The types of sediments left behind by the glacier determine soil fertility, drainage patterns, and erosion. All of Michigan's groundwater is stored in glacial sediments. Sand and gravel from outwash plains are used in industry, and clay from lake beds and till is used to seal landfills and to make pottery and tile.

Quaternary refers to a subdivision of geologic time. We are currently in the Quaternary period, and it was during this period that the Ice Age took place, resulting in the advance and retreat of glaciers. A Quaternary map shows the general distribution of sediments from the glaciers during the Quaternary period.

Quaternary maps depict surface deposits by using different colors. The map used in this investigation shows the glacial deposits that cover the Macatawa watershed in Holland, Michigan (see Figure 2.1). Five areas dominate the map. The white area represents lake deposits (lacustrine); the dotted area represents deposits of glacial till (deposited with direct contact with ice); the gray area on the left side represents dune sand; and the vertical striped area represents glacial stream deposits (outwash, material washed out of the glacier by rivers). The fat black lines on the map show the boundary of shorelines, representing historic Lake Michigan levels. The map legend gives more detail. (The color version of this map is available for download and distribution to students at *www.nsta.org/pdfs/WatershedMap.pdf*.)

---

*This investigation was adapted from a Western Michigan University Geology Department lab.

Objective

To learn how glaciers shaped a watershed.

Materials

Quaternary map of Macatawa watershed (or any watershed of your choice)

Suggested Class Preparation and Format

Student should have a basic knowledge of glaciers and glacier formations before this activity is introduced. This investigation could be used in a unit on glaciers, watersheds, or topography in an earth science class.

Teacher setup for this lab is minimal. You can use the map provided in this chapter or a quaternary map of your own watershed. Quaternary geology maps for counties in Michigan are available at *http://web4.msue.msu.edu/mnfi/data/quatgeo.cfm.* The color map for the Macatawa watershed is available for teachers to make handouts at *www.nsta.org/pdfs/WatershedMap.pdf.* To find a quaternary map for another state, you can do a Google search on the phrase "quaternary geology map for [enter your state]" or go to the website of the Association of American State Geologists (*www.stategeologists.org*) for a link to your state's geologic survey. You can also contact your state's department of natural resources for quaternary maps. If using a different map from the one here, modify the questions on the Student Handout as necessary. Print the necessary number of maps for the students and laminate before student use for longevity.

The investigation requires approximately one 50-minute class period. The students have a question sheet to answer for assessment. To complete the activity, have students discuss how glaciers shaped the Macatawa watershed or other watershed being investigated.

Answers to Questions in Student Handout

Lacustrine Deposits (Blue)

1. lacustrine sand and gravel
2. shorelines
3. no hills/flat
4. glacial Lake Michigan

Glacial Till (Green)

5. end moraines of fine-textured till
6. ground moraines of medium- to coarse-textured glacial till
7. rolling hills and low hills
8. As indicated on the quaternary map, most of the moraines in the eastern part of the watershed are end moraines. End moraines mark the greatest advance of the ice sheet.

Glacial Outwash (Pink/Purple)

9. fine to coarse sand with small gravel to heavy cobblestones
10. no hills/flat

General Questions

11. dunes
12. southwest

SCLINKS THE WORLD'S A CLICK AWAY
Topic: Changes in Glaciers
Go to: *www.scilinks.org*
Code: WAT003

Resource

Michigan Department of Environmental Quality, Geological and Land Management Division. 2003. *General geology of Michigan. www.deq.state.mi.us/documents/deq-ogs-gimdl-GGGM.pdf*

Figure 2.1 Quaternary Geology Map of the Macatawa Watershed (Color map available at *www.nsta.org/pdfs/WatershedMap.pdf.*)

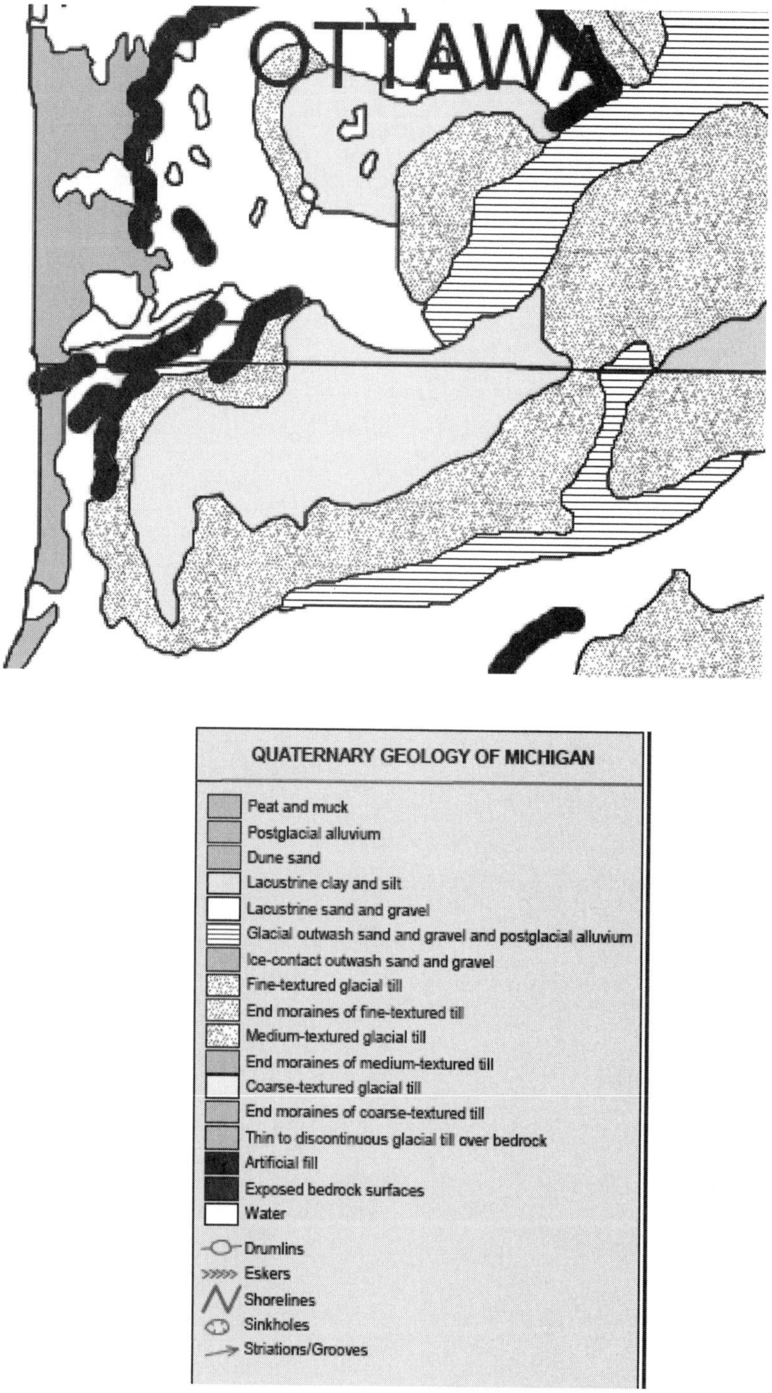

Glacial Features of a Watershed

Student Handout

Background

About 9,000 years ago the last glacier to shape the topography of Michigan retreated from the Upper Peninsula. Because glacial drift covers most of Michigan, there are very few areas where bedrock is exposed. This is also true for most of the northern portion of the United States. As the glaciers advanced and retreated, they left sediments called glacial drift in two forms, referred to as till and outwash. Sediments deposited through till are called moraines and consist of piles (hills) of unsorted materials such as sand, mud, and gravel. Till was dumped by the glacier along its leading edge. As the glacier melted, the running water left flat plain areas called outwash plains. Sediments deposited through outwash are sorted by particle size, with the finer particles being transported the farthest.

The sediments deposited by the glacier through till and outwash shaped the topography of the northern United States. Michigan glaciations not only carved out the Great Lakes but also affect our lives today in other ways. The types of sediments left behind by the glacier determine soil fertility, drainage patterns, and erosion. All of Michigan's groundwater is stored in glacial sediments. Sand and gravel from outwash plains are used in industry, and clay from lake beds and till is used to seal landfills and to make pottery and tile.

Quaternary refers to a subdivision of geologic time. We are currently in the Quaternary period, and it was during this period that the Ice Age took place, resulting in the advance and retreat of glaciers. A Quaternary map shows the general distribution of sediments from the glaciers during the Quaternary period.

Quaternary maps depict surface deposits by using different colors. Five colors dominate the map used in this investigation: blue, green, yellow, pink, and red. Blue represents lake deposits (lacustrine); green represent deposits of glacial till (deposited with direct contact with ice); yellow represents dune sand; and pink represents glacial stream deposits (outwash, material washed out of the glacier by rivers). The red lines on the map show the boundary of shorelines, and the shorelines represent historic Lake Michigan levels. The map legend gives more detail about what the colors represent.

Objective

To learn how glaciers shaped a watershed.

Name________________________________

Glacial Features of the Macatawa Watershed, Holland, Michigan

Use the map and the information in the handout to answer the following questions.

Lacustrine Deposits (Blue)

1. What type of lacustrine deposits does the watershed have?

2. What do the red lines present throughout the watershed indicate?

3. What would you expect the topography of the blue area to be like: high hills, rolling hills, low hills, or no hills/flat?

4. Based on the answers to questions 1–3, hypothesize what once covered the western part of the watershed.

Glacial Till (Green)

5. What do the darkest green colors indicate?

6. What do the medium- and light-green colors indicate?

7. What type of topography would you expect to be associated with these areas: high hills, rolling hills, low hills, or no hills/flat?

8. Based on the answers to questions 5–7, describe how the glacier formed the eastern part of the watershed.

Glacial Outwash (Pink/Purple)

9. What kinds of sediment will be found in the outwash areas?

10. What type of topography would you expect to be associated with these areas: high hills, rolling hills, low hills, no hills/flat?

General Questions

11. What landforms are represented by the yellow color?

12. In what general direction did the glacier advance over the Macatawa watershed?

CHAPTER 3

Plant Identification

Teacher Information

Background

This investigation gives students the opportunity to view the outside world and bring science into the field. Teaching students how to identify plants gives them a greater appreciation for nature, just as learning to read words lets young students begin to appreciate literature. As older students learn to identify plants, they become educated about what lives in the watershed and they develop a greater desire to preserve it. They also become familiar with invasive species that may be invading their watershed.

Many students do not like the memorization that comes with plant taxonomy, but with modest effort everybody can successfully identify by name most of the plants in their community. By the end of this field exercise, students will feel pride in their identification abilities.

Objective

To teach students common plant species that they will encounter in the watershed.

Materials

- dichotomous key (teacher's choice)
- plant specimens (for possible species, see Table 3.1 at the end of the section "Answers to Questions in Student Handout")

Suggested Class Preparation and Format

Teaching plant identification in the field can feel overwhelming, but it does not have to be if the students are prepared for the activity. It is up to you to determine how much time to spend on plant identification; as familiarity grows, this exercise can become more extensive each year. Identification can be taught alone or with other topics. For example, plant identification most likely would be included in a biology unit on plants. Plant identification would also be useful in an ecology unit with plant population counts or in a unit on invasive species.

Preparation time for this investigation will depend on your familiarity with using dichotomous keys and existing plant knowledge. A visit ahead of time to the location that the students will explore is highly recommended. Identifying all the plants could take a relatively short time or an extended time period, depending on the degree of prior knowledge of plants.

Some counties offer plant identification programs through the parks and recreation department. For example, in Ottawa County, Michigan, this department offers basic plant identification along with Dune Ecology and Winter Botany programs. You could also check with local colleges and university extension services and contact a botany professor for recommendations and information. It is likely that a local park exists with at least some of the trees already identified along the trails.

You need to select a key or book to teach plant identification. There is a plethora of dichotomous keys on the internet (e.g., *www.for.msu.edu/extension/ExtDocs/Identkey/opening.htm*), but because books are still the most portable of field equipment, using a book with a dichotomous key is the best choice. The Peterson Field Guide Series is one option for tree identification; this series is useful because the investigation is targeted toward tree identification. Once the primary knowledge is gained, herbaceous plants could be included. A nice guide that uses a dichotomous-type key for flowers is *Newcomb's Wildflower Guide* (Newcomb 1977), which covers flowers in northeastern and north-central America.

If you need to brush up on plant terminology, refer to the plant identification book(s) selected for the investigation. These books contain definitions, explanations, and pictures. The Student Handout included in this investigation contains some definitions and illustrations of very basic terms.

Use the first class period (indoors) of the identification unit to teach students what a dichotomous key is and how to use it, as well as basic plant terminology and leaf morphology. The best way to teach the terminology is to first show students a picture from the identification book and then show them several fresh specimens in the classroom (five different specimens are enough). Additional class periods indoors may be necessary to teach the basics before taking students into the field. For a wrap-up exercise indoors, have students complete their worksheets on basic plant terminology; alternatively, you can ask them to fill out the worksheets as the material is introduced. Additional plant specimens will be needed to complete the worksheet. You should use the same specimens that students were shown in class, along with some specimens they have not seen before.

Once the students have a good grasp on how to use the dichotomous key, take them outside and have them work in pairs to "key out" the plants. To keep students who finish early engaged, assign them additional species to identify. Have students keep a field notebook of all plants identified, listing habitat and major characteristics. Give the students helpful hints along the way to aid them in their memorization; for example, the peeling bark of a sycamore tree can make it look "sick"; black cherry bark looks like burnt potato chips; and the mnemonic MAD HORSES, which stands for maples, ashes, dogwoods, and horse chestnuts, can be used to identify trees that have opposite leaves. Most other tree families commonly encountered will have alternate leaves.

Plant identification can be done anywhere. City areas may have a great number and variety of tree species, but if the opportunity exists, take a field trip to a natural area near you.

SCILINKS THE WORLD'S A CLICK AWAY
Topic: How are plants classified?
Go to: *www.scilinks.org*
Code: WAT004

Tips for Identifying Plants

1. Examine the plant and determine if the leaves are opposite or alternate.
2. Look at an individual leaf and follow the leaf stalk back until you see the bud. Is the leaf compound or simple?
3. Look at the leaf shape and margins.
4. Examine the bark.
5. Use these observations with a dichotomous key to identify the plant.

Optional Extensions

- Have your students teach basic plant identification to elementary students. This provides a great assessment for the high school student and gives the elementary student a safe and supervised encounter with nature.
- Have your students make a guided walking trail by making labels for trees and plants they have identified. Index cards with information can be laminated inexpensively at a copy center.
- Have your students make a herbarium collection, which is a collection of dried plant specimens preserved on herbarium-quality paper. Instructions for preserving plant specimens and a herbarium collection rubric are included at the end of the Teacher Information section. The collection should be limited to 25 specimens; a larger collection will require too much time and effort. The rubric gives students a list of specimens to choose from; the list includes plant species in the Midwest, but feel free to make your own list using species with which you are familiar.

Answers to Questions in Student Handout

1. alternate, opposite, whorled
2. simple, palmately compound, pinnately compound
3. serrated, entire, lobed
4. See Table 3.1 for possible species and answers to this question.

Table 3.1. Possible Species of Plants to Use in Class With Students With Answers

Species Name	Opposite, Alternate or Whorled	Blade Type: Simple or Compound	Margin of Blade: entire, serrated, undulated, lobed
Any species of Maple (except Ashleaf aka Boxelder)	Opposite	Simple	Lobed (With the different species notice the shape of the sinus. Some are "V" shaped and some are "U" shaped indicating its species.
Red, Black, White, Bur Oak	Alternate (oak leaves tend to cluster)	Simple	Lobed (With the different species notice how the lobes tip differ, each difference indicating its species.)
Bitternut Hickory	Alternate	Pinnately Compound	serrate
Any species of Ash	Opposite	Pinnately Compound	Entire to serrate depending upon species
Redbud	Alternate	Simple	Entire with leaf having a heart shape
Ohio Buckeye or Horsechesnut	Opposite	Palmately Compound	serrate

References

The leaf: parts. n.d. *www.botanical-online.com/lahojaangles.htm*

Newcomb, L. 1977. *Newcomb's Wildflower Guide.* New York: Little, Brown.

Petrides, G. A. 1973. *A field guide to trees and shrubs: Northeastern and north-central United States and southeastern and south-central Canada.* New York: Peterson Field Guides. Houghton Mifflin Harcourt.

SCILINKS. THE WORLD'S A CLICK AWAY

Topic: Plant Characteristics
Go to: *www.scilinks.org*
Code: WAT005

Preserving Plant Specimens

Collecting Specimens

Select specimens for the collection that are free from any type of blemish. Use a knife or scissors to cut branches. For herbaceous plants (plants that are fleshy), cut the stem off all the way to the ground. Make sure when cutting trees or herbaceous plants that the specimen has enough leaves to determine leaf arrangement. When cutting flowers, one is sufficient. Include seeds with the specimen whenever possible. When collecting, identify the plant first before collecting it. Write the specimen's name on a piece of masking tape and wrap the tape around the stem or branch of the plant. Place the specimen in a plastic bag (such as a plastic grocery bag) with some wet paper towels. Keep the bag closed at all times. The wet paper towels keep the humidity high inside the bag to keep the plants from wilting. Plants should be pressed as soon as possible. If unable to press plants the same day, place the closed bag inside of a refrigerator. Most plants will keep for a few days.

Plant Press

Lay out the specimen on one side of a piece of a newspaper that is folded in half. Make sure the leaves are not overlapping and one leaf is turned over. Sometimes this can be tricky. Masking tape can be used to tape down branches. If using masking tape for the branches, put it on your fingers several times to take off most of the stickiness so it will not damage the specimen. Do not use masking tape on the leaves, because the tape will rip them when they are dry.

Fold the remaining half of the newspaper over the specimen. Write the species name on margin of the newspaper for later use.

Put several newspapers and, if available, a piece of corrugated cardboard in between specimens. Set heavy objects such as books on top of the stack of specimens, and wait three to five days for the specimens to dry. Try to place them in a location with little humidity, and use a fan (if available) to speed up the evaporation of the water from the plants.

Mounting Specimens

Once the plants are dry, the best thing to display them on is 11½ in. × 16½ in. herbarium paper. There are herbarium pastes that can be purchased to glue specimens to the paper, but any white glue will suffice. Never tape or staple specimens to the paper. Use your finger or a paintbrush to spread a thin layer of glue over the entire leaf surface. After covering all of the leaves on the specimen and its stem, affix the specimen to the paper. When gluing down, make sure to keep the one leaf that was turned over in the drying process so the back can be seen. Some species of plants, such as poplars or aspens, naturally turn a blackish color when dried; others tend to bubble up. These types of things are to be expected and should not cause any deduction of points on the collection. Do not cover the specimens with any type of plastic or contact paper. It is important that the viewer be able to touch the specimens for identification.

Labeling

Each specimen needs a label in the lower left corner of the herbarium paper. As shown in the sample label format below, the label should include the following information: Latin name of the plant; family name of the plant; common name of the plant; your name; date collected; city or township, county, and state where collected; specific location of collection; and habitat. The label may be typed or written in black ink.

Name of High School

Name of class, year

Latin Name ____________________

____

Family Name ____________________

Common Name ____________________

Collected by ____________________

Date of Collection ____________________

City or Township, County, and State of Collection

____

Specific Location of Collection ____________________

____

Habitat ____________________

Turning in the Collection

The collection must be in alphabetical order according to family. Prepare a table of contents for the collection that consists of the family name, Latin name, common name, and page number for each specimen. Place specimens with the table of contents and the rubric on top in a brown paper bag, and turn the collection in to the teacher.

Herbarium Collection Rubric

Name______________________________

The herbarium collection is due on ____________. Every day (not class day) the collection is late, 10 points will be deducted. Two (2) points will be awarded for correctly identifying the specimen and 2 points will be awarded for quality of specimen and accuracy of information, giving a maximum of 4 points per specimen for a maximum total of 100 points.

Include 25 of any species listed below in your collection. Please check off the species included in the collection.

- ☐ maple (any species)
- ☐ sumac (any species)
- ☐ pawpaw
- ☐ Queen Anne's lace
- ☐ yarrow
- ☐ knapweed (any species)
- ☐ aster (any species)
- ☐ touch-me-not
- ☐ alder (any species)
- ☐ birch (any species)
- ☐ American hornbeam
- ☐ hop hornbeam
- ☐ milkweed (any species)
- ☐ dogwood (any species)
- ☐ redbud
- ☐ Kentucky coffee tree
- ☐ bird's-foot trefoil
- ☐ clover (any species)
- ☐ cow vetch
- ☐ American beech
- ☐ oak (any species)
- ☐ ginkgo
- ☐ witch hazel
- ☐ American chestnut
- ☐ Ohio buckeye
- ☐ horse chestnut
- ☐ hickory (any species)
- ☐ walnut (any species)
- ☐ catnip
- ☐ spicebush
- ☐ sassafras
- ☐ tulip tree
- ☐ black gum
- ☐ sweet gum
- ☐ ash (any species)
- ☐ sycamore
- ☐ cherry (any species)
- ☐ swamp rose
- ☐ aspen (any species)
- ☐ elm (any species)
- ☐ basswood
- ☐ blue vervain
- ☐ Virginia creeper
- ☐ boneset
- ☐ joe-pye weed
- ☐ purple loosestrife
- ☐ evening primrose

Plant Identification

Student Handout

Background

In this investigation you will identify different types of trees by learning plant morphology terms and how to use a dichotomous key. Being able to identify common plants you encounter every day will make you more aware of the diversity that exists among plants.

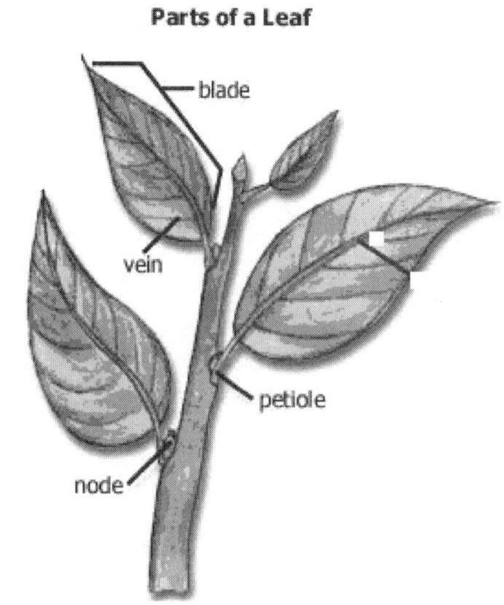

Typically, a leaf consists of a flattened laminar portion (the blade), and a leaf stalk (the petiole), which attaches it to the stem (see illustration). The node is the point of leaf attachment where buds can be seen. The laminar (thin and platelike) shape allows the leaf to absorb light energy and allows for gas exchange.

Although the internal construction of the many thousands of angiosperm (flowering plant) species is similar, the external form of the leaf is highly variable. This variability is often critical to the identification of the plant. There are three major features to look for when identifying the leaf of a plant:

1. the arrangement of the leaves—alternate, opposite, or whorled,
2. the type of leaf blade—simple or compound, and
3. the margin of the leaf blade.

Arrangement of Leaves

The leaf may be attached directly opposite another leaf, or it may alternate attachments with leaves on the other side, or it may have many leaves that "whorl" around the stem. You can determine whether a leaf is opposite, alternate, or whorled simply by examining the arrangement of the leaves on the stem (see illustrations p. 25).

Type of Leaf

A simple leaf consists of a single blade. A compound leaf consists of a blade composed of a number of separate, leaflike parts known as leaflets. When leaflets branch off all the way along a central axis (rachis), the leaf is said to be pinnately compound. Pinnately compound leaves may be once, twice, or thrice pinnately compound depending on the number of leaflets branching off along the petiole. When the leaflets are all attached at a common point near the tip of the petiole, the leaf is said to be palmately compound. The illustration below shows simple and compound leaves.

Types of Leaves

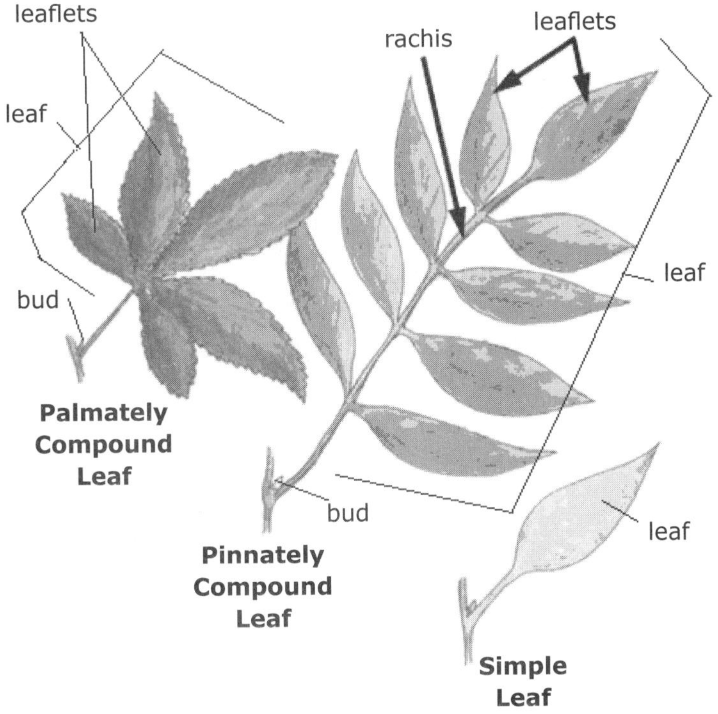

SCI LINKS
THE WORLD'S A CLICK AWAY

Topic: Plant Structure
Go to: www.scilinks.org
Code: WAT006

You can distinguish whether a leaf is simple or compound by examining its stem and nearest neighboring leaves. Note that buds occur on the branch at the base of the petiole of leaves and do not occur at the base of leaflets. Also, the blades of simple leaves are oriented in many different planes on the stem, whereas the blades of leaflets all occur in the same plane.

In many angiosperms, the leaf has a pair of small appendages (stipules), attached to the base of the petiole. Don't confuse these stipules with the buds.

Margin of the Leaf

The margins of the leaf blade for different species are quite variable. They can typically be described in one of four ways (see illustration below):

- Smooth/entire—the entire edge of the leaf is smooth.
- Toothed/serrated—the edge has teeth or shallow indentations along it.
- Undulated—the leaf has wavy edges.
- Lobed—the entire leaf has large indentations (e.g., an oak leaf). The indentation is referred to as the sinus and the leaf matter that juts out is the lobe.

Smooth/entire Toothed/serrated Undulated Lobed

Objective

To learn about common plant species in your watershed.

Materials

- dichotomous key
- plant specimens

Name______________________________

Plant Identification Worksheet

1. Label the illustrations below as opposite, alternate, or whorled.

2. Label the illustrations below as simple, palmately compound. or pinnately compound. On the pinnately compound leaf, label the rachis and leaflet. On the simple leaf, label the sinus and the lobe.

3. Label each of the illustrations below as smooth/entire, toothed/serrated, or lobed.

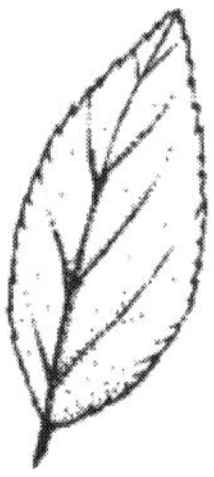

4. Use the dichotomous key to identify the specimens provided, and fill in the table below as you complete the identification.

Species Name	Opposite, Alternate or Whorled	Blade Type: Simple or Compound	Margin of Blade: Entire, Serrated, Undulated, Lobed

CHAPTER 4

Wetland Delineation

Teacher Information*

Background

Wetlands are usually found in low areas, next to rivers, lakes, or streams and in areas where clay soil is abundant; or on slopes where the groundwater seeps. They can also occur wherever the water table is high enough to inundate the soil on a regular basis. Wetlands can be described by a host of other words, which perhaps indicates how common they used to be: bogs, peats, marshes, swamps, fens, quagmires, mires, morasses, sloughs, sumps, and so on.

For the most part, early settlers of this country did not embrace wetlands. "Too thick to plow and too dry to drink" was an old adage farmers used to describe wetlands. Pioneers usually considered wetlands to be useless and a waste of good land. Expressions that are still common in our vocabulary today shed some light on how people used to view wetlands. Take, for example, the negative connotations surrounding the word *swamp*. How often do we say "I'm swamped with work"? How about the word *bog*, as in "bogged down"? These commonly used phrases help to perpetuate the negative view many people have of wetlands.

When the settlers first arrived in many areas of the country, the first thing they often worked together to do was drain the wetlands. Once the wetlands were drained, towns could be started and land converted into arable property, which was much more valuable to the settlers. Many wetland areas were destroyed to make way for farmland or cities, and only a few wetland areas survived. Most experts estimate that more than 50% of wetlands in this country have been destroyed. Even if they were not intentionally destroyed, many wetlands today may be unrecognizable because of human disturbance, which makes the determination of their boundaries extremely difficult. For example, using too much water in a specific location can lower the water table and change wetlands significantly. The federal government encouraged the destruction of wetlands with their many Swamp Land Acts, and it was not until the 1930s that a public effort was made to stop their destruction. This effort was made by duck hunters, who were the first group to take notice of the value wetlands serve in an ecosystem; using funds from the sale of duck stamps, they began to buy wetland habitat for preservation (Mitsch and Gosselink 2000).

*The idea for this investigation was provided by Martin Landes in 2005.

We know now that wetlands are a critical part of our ecological health because they provide water flow control and water quality improvements (by filtering the water). In addition, wetlands are an irreplaceable habitat for many flora and fauna. Since the late 1970s, a variety of state and federal laws have been enacted to protect the remaining wetlands in the United States Typically the laws are designed to prevent wetland "development" of any kind, without some mitigation elsewhere. Of course, this has led to numerous situations where different people and organizations have different opinions of what is really a wetland area. To this end, the federal government and each state has independently defined what exactly constitutes a wetland. Although there are multiple definitions, and they can also vary with time as different laws are modified, there is now a set of criteria generally accepted to delineate a wetland.

Learning how to delineate a wetland using official criteria can be an enlightening experience for all students and teachers. Wetland delineation is not black and white; there is a lot of gray area. There is an appreciable uncertainty in any student delineation study the first time it is done, but by becoming familiar with the process and comparing results between groups (and even between years) confidence in the technique can be established. The following paragraphs describe the delineation method used by Michigan Department of Environmental Quality (n.d.) and each wetland indicator.

In Michigan, the identification of wetlands is determined by hydrophytic (water-loving) vegetation and hydrology (the study of water flow). When hydrologic indicators are absent, the soil is analyzed to determine if it is a hydric soil, which indicates wetland hydrology. Of course, all three of these indicators are interconnected. The hydrology determines the hydric soil which determines the vegetation and so forth (Mitsch and Gosselink 2000).

Hydrophytic vegetation refers to plants that are adapted to the anoxic and wet conditions of a wetland. If an area is dominated by plants that are hydrophytic, then that satisfies the first definition of a wetland. According to the 1989 interagency federal manual for wetland delineation (Federal Interagency Committee for Wetland Delineation 1989), which is referenced in Ralph Tiner's *Wetland Indicators* (1999), plant dominance is determined per stratum where "dominant species are the most abundant plant species (when ranked in descending order of abundance and cumulatively totaled) that immediately exceeds 50% of the total dominance measure for the stratum, plus any additional species comprising 20% or more of the total dominance measure for the stratum" (Tiner 1999, p. 111) This is referred to as the "50/20 rule." A stratum refers to a layer of vegetation such a herbaceous stratum or sapling stratum.

To help determine hydrophytic plant dominance, the U.S. Fish and Wildlife Service has divided plants into five categories based on the likelihood of finding them in a wetland area (U.S. Department of Agriculture, Natural Resources Conservation Service n.d.):

- Obligate wetland (OBL) plants occur in wetlands greater than 99% of the time and less than 1% of the time in nonwetlands.
- Facultative wetland (FACW) plants occur in wetlands 67%–99% of the time and in nonwetlands 1%–33% of the time.
- Facultative (FAC) plants occur in both wetlands and nonwetlands 34%–66% of the time.
- Facultative upland (FACU) plants occur in wetlands 1%–33% of the time and in uplands (nonwetlands) 67%–99% of the time.
- Obligate upland (nonwetland) (UPL) plants occur in uplands greater than 99% of the time.

Pluses and minuses are also used to indicate the upper and lower portions of the range, respectively. An example would be FAC+, which indicates that the species may occur in wetlands 51%–67% of the time. Plant species that fall in the OBL and FACW+ categories are the best hydrophytic indicators of the presence of a wetland. When this type of vegetation is dominant, the area should be recognized as a wetland (Tiner, 1999).

When the plants do not clearly indicate a wetland, the next step is to look for positive indicators of wetland *hydrology*. Despite what most people think, a wetland does not have to have standing water. The soil only has to be saturated within 30 cm of the soil surface for 14 days or longer during the growing season in most years. To determine if hydrology is present, dig a hole at least 46 cm deep. If the hole fills in with water, this is an indicator of wetland hydrology. Another indicator of wetland hydrology is an oxidized rhizosphere (the soil zone around plant roots), in which the soil near the plant roots contains mottles (discolorations) or the trees display drift lines (debris left on a tree trunk from a high-water mark), water-stained leaves, water marks, and surfaced scoured areas. (Surfaced scoured areas are usually areas next to a river or stream [floodplain area] that have experienced erosion of sediments) . Hydrology is highly variable and unreliable because it is greatly affected by time of year and weather. One of the best indicators of hydrology is the presence of hydric soils (Cwikiel 2003).

Hydric soils are characterized by being a bluish-greenish-grayish color referred to as gley. Interspersed throughout the gley, mottles will often be present. Mottles are spots of red formed from the oxidation of iron particles with oxygen dissolved in water—basically, it is the soil becoming "rusty."

Objective

To delineate the boundaries of an area in a watershed and categorize it as a wetland or not a wetland by examining the vegetation, soil, and hydrology (the same parameters that government agencies use to delineate wetlands).

Materials Needed Per Group

- area to be delineated (You can use one that is known to be a wetland or, to make the delineation more difficult, land that is near a known wetland.)
- plant species list indicating wetland obligate and facultative status
- shovel
- 10 flags for marking wetland boundary
- soil auger (optional)
- soil color chart (optional)
- wetland plant identification guides (optional)
- hand calculator for determining dominance percentage (optional)
- one or more pairs of waders (optional, but can be very helpful; advise students to wear footwear and clothing that can get wet and dirty—often field gear can be ruined by exposure to muddy water!)
- insect repellent (optional, but can be very helpful depending on the time of year)

Suggested Class Preparation and Format

The plant identification investigation in Chapter 3 should be completed before beginning this investigation. Students should be familiar with common wetland and upland plants by sight. This investigation would be useful in a biology course when studying different ecosystems, including wetlands, and could also be used to reinforce the plant identification activities.

Teacher preparation is minimal. You need to select an area to be delineated, and (as noted in the materials list), you need to provide a list of plants with wetland indicator status. There are several lists available on the internet for each region of the country, and the U.S. Fish and Wildlife Service has links to other resources at their National Wetlands Inventory web page *www.fws.gov/nwi/Plants/plants.htm*. Several other good sites can be found by searching the internet for "wetland plant inventory."

You may give students a traditional set of instructions (Student Handout A) or use a more open-ended exploratory laboratory, in which only the methods are explained and students must design their own set of experiments and methods (Student Handout B). The delineation of wetlands by legal standards is a difficult task to do correctly, and there may be many "shades of gray" encountered by students in performing this activity.

Have students split into teams and direct them to use the indicators they have learned to decide where to put their flags to mark the boundary of the wetland. After the wetland has been delineated, a discussion of why delineation is important should be held. During this discussion, refer to the background information provided in this investigation as needed; you may also want to bring to class a recent article on fines incurred by people who have destroyed wetlands to make way for construction projects.

SCILINKS THE WORLD'S A CLICK AWAY

Topic: Wetlands
Go to: *www.scilinks.org*
Code: WAT007

Procedure

1. Have the students split into teams.
2. The first indicator that should be examined is vegetation. Students should first look at how the species of vegetation changes from the wetland area to the upland area. The students should see 100% hydrophytic vegetation in the wetland area; as they move outward from the wetland boundary into the upland area, this percentage will decrease as upland species take over. Have the students do one population count per stratum and record plant species and status. To do this, stake out 1 square meter of space to be evaluated with a 4 m rope threaded through the plants and tied to itself and then stretched into a square. "Percent cover" is usually the easiest population count to do, and a good rule of thumb is that the size of your fist represents 1% in a square meter plot. A very useful reference on population sampling is *Invasion Ecology* by Marianne Krasny (2002).
3. Once students have recorded their population counts, they can apply the 50/20 rule or another, much easier method that uses weighted averages; the latter method was developed by Wentworth and Johnson in 1986 (cited in Tiner 1999). In this method, each wetland plant status is given a value called the ecological index, where OBL = 1, FACW = 2, FAC = 3, FACU = 4, and UPL = 5. The first step in calculating the weighted average is to find the product of percent cover and ecological index for each plant. The weighted average can then be calculated by dividing the total products by the total percent covers.

   If the weighted average equals 2.0 or less, the area is considered a wetland. If the average is 2.1–2.5, the area has a high probability of being a wetland but hydrology should be checked to confirm status. If the average is 2.6–3.4, this information is not enough to determine absence or presence of a wetland; other indicators must be analyzed. If the average is 3.5–4, the area is probably an upland, but hydrology should be checked to confirm status. If the average is 4.1 or above, the area is not a wetland and is considered an upland (Tiner 1999).

Table 4.1 provides a sample calculation of the weighted average for a herbaceous stratum. In this example, the total products (162) divided by the total percent covers (100) is 1.62. Therefore, this area would be considered a wetland because its weighted average is less than 2.

Table 4.1. Sample Calculation of Weighted Average for a Herbaceous Stratum

Genus/species	Common Name	% Cover in Plot	Ecological Index	Product (% Cover × Ecological Index)
Impatiens capensis	Spotted touch-me-not	50	2	100
Eupatorium maculatum	Joe-pye weed	30	1	30
Asclepias incarnata	Swamp milkweed	5	1	5
Carex gynandra	Nodding sedge	5	2	10
Eupatorium perfoliatum	Common boneset	5	2	10
Lobelia cardinalis	Cardinalflower	3	1	3
Solidago gigantea	Late goldenrod	2	2	4
Total		100	N/A	162
Weighted average:	1.62	Wetland status:	Yes (less than 2)	

Adapted from Tiner 1999.

After students have completed step 3 they only need to finish this procedure for strata that had a weighted average greater than 2.0, although you may want them to do a complete procedure for all strata.

4. Tell students to look for signs of hydrology like water-stained leaves and surfaced scoured area.
5. Have students dig a hole 46 cm deep and watch to see if it fills with water, which would indicate wetland hydrology.
6. Have students use the soil auger or shovel to take soil samples, starting in the upland area and going toward the wetland area. As they do this they should see the change in the soil. The upland soil typically will be brown and dry. As they approach the wetland they should see the hydric soil. The hydric soil will be a bluish-greenish-grayish color called gley. Gley will typically have vertical streaking of a dark brown color and red mottles. Examples of gley in soils can be found online at
   - *http://content.answers.com/main/content/wp/en/thumb/1/1e/200px-Gleysoil.JPG*
   - *http://sciences.aum.edu/BI/BI4523/student/Christa/gley.gif*
   - *www.soilandwater.co.uk/pics/Sandy%20Gley%20large.jpeg*
   - *www.w3.a300.pl/Soil.html*

The soil will contain a lot of moisture. Hydric soils are the best indicator for wetland hydrology. All soil auger or shovel holes should be refilled once all the observations have been made. Unfilled holes are a safety hazard for students collecting additional data.

If there is enough time, have the students mark the boundary with flags using their data.

Optional Extension

Students can check each other's boundaries, which will bring up an interesting discussion of how wetland delineation is subjective. Students could also go online to Google Earth and obtain aerial images of their wetland site; they can use these images to determine the boundary with topography and then go into the field and use the primary indicators listed in the tables in Student Handout A.

Answers to Questions in Student Handouts

1. Today wetland delineation is important mostly for property owners who wish to know where they are allowed to build.
2. Wetlands play an important role in ecosystems. They provide habitat for many organisms, provide rest stops for migratory birds, provide flood storage, recharge groundwater, filter sediments, and improve water quality.
3. Depending on the issues that occur in specific watersheds, some general answers are provide flood storage, filter sediments, or improve water quality.
4. Wetland delineation is very subjective. Boundaries may differ widely.
5. Hydrology determines the soil and vegetation: excess water will yield hydric soils, whereas little water will yield dry upland soils. The amount of water and the type of soil directly determine the kinds of plants that can grow. Only hydrophytic plants can tolerate the wet conditions produced in a wetland. The soil and vegetation both affect the hydrology.

References

Cwikiel, W. 2003. *Michigan wetlands—yours to protect: A citizen's guide to wetland protection.* Petoskey, MI: Tip of the Mitt Watershed Council.

Federal Interagency Committee for Wetland Delineation (FICWD). 1989. *Federal manual for identifying and delineating jurisdictional wetlands.* Cooperative Technical Publication. Washington, DC: U.S. Army Corps of Engineers, U.S. Environmental Protection Agency, U.S. Fish and Wildlife Service, and U.S.D.A. Soil Conservation Service.

Krasny, M. E., and the Environmental Inquiry Team. 2002. *Invasion ecology: Teacher's guide.* Arlington, VA: NSTA Press.

Michigan Department of Environmental Quality. n.d. Wetland identification: Hydrology, vegetation, and soils. *www.michigan.gov/deq/0,1607,7-135-3313_3687-10332--,00.html*

Mitsch, W. J., and J. G. Gosselink. 2000. *Wetlands,* 3rd ed. New York: John Wiley and Sons.

Tiner, R. W. 1999. *Wetland indicators: A guide to wetland identification, delineation, classification, and mapping.* Boca Raton, FL: Lewis Publishers.

U.S. Department of Agriculture, Natural Resources Conservation Service. n.d. Wetland indicator status. *http://plants.usda.gov/wetinfo.html*

Wetland Delineation

Student Handout A

Background

Wetlands are usually found in low areas, next to rivers, lakes, or streams and in areas where clay soil is abundant; or on slopes where the groundwater seeps. They can also occur wherever the water table is high enough to inundate the soil on a regular basis. Wetlands can be described by a host of other words, which perhaps indicates how common they used to be: bogs, peats, marshes, swamps, fens, quagmires, mires, morasses, sloughs, sumps, and so on.

For the most part, early settlers of this country did not like wetlands. "Too thick to plow and too dry to drink" was an old adage farmers used to describe wetlands. Pioneers usually considered wetlands to be useless and a waste of good land. Expressions that are still common in our vocabulary today shed some light on how people used to view wetlands. Take, for example, the negative connotations surrounding the word *swamp*. How often do we say "I'm swamped with work"? How about the word *bog*, as in "bogged down"? These commonly used phrases help to perpetuate the negative view many people have of wetlands.

When the settlers first arrived in many areas of the country, the first thing they often worked together to do was drain the wetlands. Once the wetlands were drained, towns could be started and land converted into arable property, which was much more valuable to the settlers. Many wetland areas were destroyed to make way for farmland or cities, and only a few wetland areas survived. Most experts estimate that more than 50% of wetlands in this country have been destroyed. Even if they weren't intentionally destroyed, many wetlands today may be unrecognizable because of human disturbance, which makes the determination of their boundaries extremely difficult. For example, simply using too much water in a specific location can lower a water table and change wetlands significantly.

We know now that wetlands are a critical part of our ecological health because they provide water flow control and water quality improvements (by filtering the water). In addition, they are an irreplaceable habitat for many flora and fauna.

Objective

To delineate the boundaries of an area in a watershed and categorize it as a wetland or not a wetland by examining the vegetation, soil, and hydrology (the same parameters that government agencies use to delineate wetlands).

Materials Needed Per Group

- area to be delineated
- plant species list indicating wetland status (e.g., *www.michigan.gov/deq/0,1607,7-135-3313_3687-10375--,00.html*)
- shovel
- 10 flags for marking wetland boundary
- soil auger (optional)
- soil color chart (optional)
- wetland plant identification guides (optional)
- hand calculator for determining dominance percentage (optional)
- one or more pair of waders (optional)
- insect repellent (optional)

Procedure

1. Split into teams.
2. The first indicator that should be examined is vegetation. Look at how the species of vegetation changes from the wetland area to the upland area. Perform one population count per stratum and record plant species and status (i.e., wetland obligate [OBL], wetland facultative [FACW], facultative [FAC], upland facultative [FACU], or upland obligate [UPL]). To do this, stake out 1 square meter of space to be evaluated with a 4 m rope threaded through the plants and tied to itself and then stretched into a square. "Percent cover" is usually the easiest population count to do, and a good rule of thumb to follow is the size of your fist represents 1% in a square meter plot (while standing upright and holding you fist at arm's length down toward the ground below you). Record your data and assign each plant its corresponding wetland indicator status OBL, FACW, FAC, FACU, or UPL.
3. Using the ecological index values OBL = 1, FACW = 2, FAC = 3, FACU = 4, and UPL = 5, calculate the overall plant status for the area by taking a weighted average of the species surveyed. The first step in calculating the weighted average is to find the product of percent cover and ecological index for each plant. The weighted average can then be calculated by dividing the total products by the total percent covers. If the weighted average equals 2.0 or less, the area is considered a wetland. If the average is 2.1–2.5, the area has a high probability of being a wetland but hydrology should be checked to confirm status. If the average is 2.6–3.4, this information is not enough to determine absence or presence of a wetland; other indicators must be analyzed. If the average is 3.5–4, the area is probably an upland, but hydrology should be checked to confirm status. If the average is 4.1 or above, the area is not a wetland and is considered an upland.

Sample Calculations

Genus/species	Common Name	% Cover in Plot	Ecological Index	Product (% Cover × Ecological Index)
Impatiens capensis	Spotted touch-me-not	50		
Eupatorium maculatum	Joe-pye weed	30		
Asclepias incarnata	Swamp milkweed	5		
Carex gynandra	Nodding sedge	5		
Eupatorium perfoliatum	Common boneset	5		
Lobelia cardinalis	Cardinalflower	3		
Solidago gigantea	Late goldenrod	2		
Total		100	N/A	
Weighted average:		Wetland status:		

4. If the weighted average is greater than 2.0, look for signs of recent hydrologic presence such as water-stained leaves, surfaced scoured area, and detritus around the base of tree stumps.
5. Dig a hole 46 cm deep and watch to see if it fills with water. Record observations.
6. Use the soil auger or shovel to take soil samples, starting in the upland area and going toward the wetland area. Record soil observations.
7. (Optional, if there is enough time) Mark the wetland boundary with flags using your data.

Name________________________________

Wetland Delineation Data Tables and Questions

1. Why is wetland delineation important?
2. Why are wetlands valuable?
3. What important function do wetlands provide in a watershed?
4. Is it possible for different people to come up with different locations for the wetland boundary? Why or why not?
5. Explain how hydrology, hydric soils, and hydrophytic vegetation are all interconnected.

Vegetation: Herbaceous Stratum

Genus/species	Common Name	% Cover	Indicator Status / Ecological Index Number	Product (% Cover × Ecological Index)
Total			N/A	
Weighted average:		Wetland status:		

Vegetation: Sapling Stratum

Genus/species	Common Name	% Cover	Indicator Status / Ecological Index Number	Product (% Cover × Ecological Index)
Total			N/A	
Weighted average:		Wetland status:		

Vegetation: Overstory Stratum

Genus/species	Common Name	% Cover	Indicator Status / Ecological Index Number	Product (% Cover × Ecological Index)
Total			N/A	
Weighted Average:		Status of wetland:		

Hydrology: Herbaceous Stratum (requires one primary indicator or two secondary indicators)

Primary Indicators	Secondary Indicators
☐ Visible observation of water (depth __ inches)	☐ Oxidized rhizosphere in upper 12 inches
☐ Visible observation of soil saturation (depth __ inches)	☐ Water-stained leaves
☐ Hydric soils (gley color and mottles)	☐ Confirmation that soil profile matches hydric soil list
☐ Watermarks	☐ Bare soil areas
☐ Drift lines	☐ Morphological plant adaptations (check below)
☐ Sediment deposits	
☐ Drainage patterns within wetlands	

Source: Adapted from Michigan Department of Environmental Quality Wetland Identification Data Form at *www.deq.state.mi.us/documents/deq-water-wetlands-wetlanddataform.pdf.*

Hydrology: Sapling Stratum (requires one primary indicator or two secondary indicators)

Primary Indicators	Secondary Indicators
☐ Visible observation of water (depth __ inches)	☐ Oxidized rhizosphere in upper 12 inches
☐ Visible observation of soil saturation (Depth __ inches)	☐ Water-stained leaves
☐ Hydric soils (gley color and mottles)	☐ Confirmation that soil profile matches hydric soil list
☐ Watermarks	☐ Bare soil areas
☐ Drift lines	☐ Morphological plant adaptations (check below)
☐ Sediment deposits	
☐ Drainage patterns within wetlands	

Source: Adapted from Michigan Department of Environmental Quality Wetland Identification Data Form at *www.deq.state.mi.us/documents/deq-water-wetlands-wetlanddataform.pdf.*

Hydrology: Overstory Stratum (requires one primary indicator or two secondary indicators)

Primary Indicators	Secondary Indicators
☐ Visible observation of water (depth __ inches)	☐ Oxidized rhizosphere in upper 12 inches
☐ Visible observation of soil saturation (depth __ inches)	☐ Water-stained leaves
☐ Hydric soils (gley color and mottles)	☐ Confirmation that soil profile matches hydric soil list
☐ Watermarks	☐ Bare soil areas
☐ Drift lines	☐ Morphological plant adaptations (check below)
☐ Sediment deposits	
☐ Drainage patterns within wetlands	

Source: Adapted from Michigan Department of Environmental Quality Wetland Identification Data Form at *www.deq.state.mi.us/documents/deq-water-wetlands-wetlanddataform.pdf.*

Soil Profile Notes: Herbaceous Stratum

Depth (inches)	Soil Color	Mottle Color	Texture (sandy, loam, etc.)	Observations

Soil Profile Notes: Sapling Stratum

Depth (inches)	Soil Color	Mottle Color	Texture (sandy, loam, etc.)	Observations

Soil Profile Notes: Overstory Stratum

Depth (inches)	Soil Color	Mottle Color	Texture (sandy, loam, etc.)	Observations

Wetland Delineation

Student Handout B

Objective

To delineate the boundaries of an area in a watershed and categorize it as a wetland or not a wetland by examining the vegetation, soil, and hydrology (the same parameters that government agencies use to delineate wetlands).

In this investigation you will delineate a wetland using the information you have learned in the classroom. The first step in designing this field study is to determine how you will identify the wetland boundaries. Once you have a written procedure, you will go into the field and test it.

Think about the following questions as you prepare your investigation:

1. What types of data should be collected?
2. Which indicator will you test first?
3. What secondary indicators will be observed?
4. What data will you use to determine the boundary?

Write down a step-by-step procedure, and create a data table you will use to fill in the results. Gather the equipment you need to take into the field after the teacher has approved your procedure. When data collection is complete, use flags to mark your wetland boundary and then answer the questions at the end of this handout on a separate sheet of paper. Turn in your procedure along with your data tables.

Materials

- area to be delineated
- plant species list indicating wetland status (e.g., *www.michigan.gov/deq/0,1607,7-135-3313_3687-10375--,00.html*)
- shovel
- 10 flags for marking wetland boundary
- soil auger (optional)
- soil color chart (optional)
- wetland plant identification guides (optional)
- hand calculator for determining dominance percentage (optional)
- one or more pair of waders (optional)
- insect repellent (optional)

Methods

Determining Hydrophytic Vegetation Status

Using the ecological index values OBL = 1, FACW = 2, FAC = 3, FACU = 4, and UPL = 5, calculate the overall plant status for the area. The first step in calculating the weighted average is to find the product of percent cover and ecological index for each plant. The weighted average can then be calculated by dividing the total products by the total percent covers.

If the weighted average equals 2.0 or less, the area is considered a wetland. If the average is 2.1–2.5, the area has a high probability of being a wetland, but hydrology should be checked to confirm status. If the average is 2.6–3.4, this information is not enough to determine absence or presence of a wetland; other indicators must be analyzed. If the average is 3.5–4, the area is probably an upland, but hydrology should be checked to confirm status. If the average is 4.1 or above, the area is not a wetland and is considered an upland. Determine hydrophytic vegetation status per stratum.

Determining Hydrology

Dig a hole 46 cm deep and watch to see if it fills with water. Record observations. Look for water marks, water-stained leaves, bare soil, and surfaced scoured areas.

Determining Hydric Soils in Nonsandy Areas

Use the soil auger or shovel to take soil samples, starting in the upland area and going toward the wetland area. Look for organic soil, sulfur odor, gley color, and mottles.

Determining Hydric Soils in Sandy Areas

Use the soil auger or shovel to take soil samples, starting in the upland area and going toward the wetland area. Look for organic material in the surface horizon and vertical streaking of organic material in other soil layers.

Name________________________________

Wetland Delineation Questions

1. Why is wetland delineation important?

____

____

____

2. What are the values of wetlands?

____

____

____

3. What important function do wetlands provide in our watershed?

____

____

____

4. Is it possible for different people to come up with different locations for the wetland boundary? Why or why not?

____

____

____

5. Explain how hydrology, hydric soils, and hydrophytic vegetation are all interconnected.

____

____

____

CHAPTER 5

Measuring Plant Allelopathy

Teacher Information*

Background

Native species are organisms that have evolved in the land area in which they currently reside; these species have defenses to protect their population size and natural predators to limit their population size. *Non-native, exotic, alien, nonindigenous,* and *foreign* are all words to describe an organism that is not original to the ecosystem. A non-native species is labeled as invasive when it affects the native plants and/or animals negatively. Invasive species may harm an ecosystem by displacing native species, thereby reducing the biodiversity of an area. When biodiversity is reduced, animals may not have enough food resources or places for habitat, which could lead to native plants being extirpated.

An example of an aquatic invasive in the Great Lakes watershed is the zebra mussel (*Dreissena polymorpha*). This invasive was originally transported to the Great Lakes by ballast water. Zebra mussels attach to any hard substrate and therefore effectively plug intake pipes, affecting boaters and utilities everywhere in the Great Lakes. Another well-known invasive is purple loosestrife (*Lythrum salicaria*). Purple loosestrife was probably first brought to the East Coast in the 1800s by ballast water and sheep fleece. Gardeners helped it spread westward, and now it is found in all of the 48 contiguous states except Florida. Purple loosestrife outcompetes other plants for sunlight and space in its wetland habitat. Each mature purple loosestrife plant can produce 2.5 million seeds, which aid it in completely taking over an area (Hart et al. 2000).

Zebra mussels and purple loosestrife are just two examples of invasive species that have become a huge problem in the United States. The production of large numbers of seeds is not the only advantage possessed by invasive species. They may lack predators to eat them, and often they are readily dispersed by wind, water, or humans. *Allelopathy,* which is defined as one species inhibiting another's growth by releasing chemicals with adverse effects, can be another weapon in the arsenal of an invasive species (Ramey 2005).

---

*Dr. Kathy Winnett-Murray of Hope College in Holland, Michigan, provided the idea for the experiment in this investigation.

Many common native and invasive plants exhibit allelopathic tendencies. Allelopathic plants may release chemicals from their leaves, roots, stems, flowers, or fruits, and the chemicals are typically found in the soil surrounding the plant. The chemical released may affect the surrounding plants by inhibiting shoot and/or root growth and nutrient uptake or by attacking naturally occurring symbiotic relationships, and these effects of the chemical destroy the plant's source of nutrients. There also is some research suggesting that these chemicals affect animals (Oudhia 2001).

Allelopathic effects vary from plant to plant, and an allelochemical that has a negative effect on one plant species may have a positive effect on a different plant species. In one experiment, *Leucaena leucocephala*, the so-called miracle tree, reduced the yield of wheat nearby but increased the yield of rice (Ferguson and Rathinasabapathi 2003). In addition, the allelochemicals released by one species may not affect all species equally. One example is juglone (5 hydroxy-1,4-napthoquinone), which originates from black walnut trees (*Juglans nigra*); this chemical has been shown to inhibit the growth of tomato, pepper, and eggplant but not beets, carrot, corn, cherry, catalpa, and Virginia creeper. Each plant shows varying degrees of susceptibility to juglone (Rivenshield 2006). Another example of an allelopathic chemical is a coumarin compound called 3, 4-dihydrocoumarin (see Figure 5.1) found in yellow sweet clover (*Melilotus officinalis*). Plants use coumarin to protect themselves when injured; the chemical inhibits the growth of fungus and deters terrestrial beetles. Coumarin is active in plant metabolism and may delay seed germination. Furthermore, coumarin can be used as an anti-inflammatory, an anticoagulant, and an antimicrobial in humans (Ojala 2001).

Plants that typically do not show allelopathy include all species of maple (*Acer spp.*), oak (*Quercus spp.*), and ash (*Fraxinus spp.*); gray-headed coneflower (*Ratibida pinnata*), heath aster (*Aster pilosus*), and New England aster (*Aster novae-angliae*).

Figure 5.1.

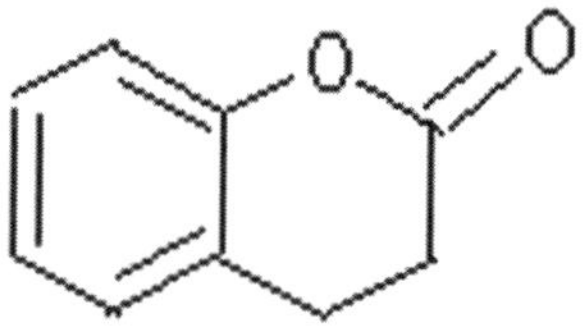

Objective

To compare the allelopathic effects of native and non-native plants on the germination of seeds.

Materials Needed Per Group

- a native and a non-native plant (Specimens collected the day before class should be stored in ziplock bags and kept in a refrigerator overnight.)
- 6 petri dishes
- moistened paper towels
- 12 pieces of size 3 filter paper or paper towels cut to fit a petri dish

- 120 lettuce seeds (Any seed that germinates in 2–3 days is fine. Seeds are available in the plant and garden section of the supermarket. It is advisable not to use old seed packages because the percentage that germinates will be lower.)
- hot plate (Have students share as needed.)
- 2 beakers
- 1 100 ml graduated cylinder
- 1 10 ml graduated cylinder
- 1 6"× 6" piece of cheesecloth
- deionized (DI) water, or any type of purified water
- Texas Instruments (TI) graphing calculator
- gloves (optional)

Suggested Class Preparation and Format

Setup time will be minimal. You may give students a traditional set of instructions (Student Handout A) or use a more open-ended exploratory laboratory, in which only the methods are explained and students must design their own set of experiments and methods (Student Handout B). This investigation would fit in well during a unit on ecology and relationships between organisms in the community. The investigation could also be used when studying invasive species and their effects on the environment in biology.

A typical approach is to provide an introduction to allelopathy in the first class period of the investigation. In subsequent class periods, the students will collect and identify plants outside during class time; alternatively, they can bring in plants from home and identify them during class. The students will need to conduct background research to find out if the selected plants are native or invasive and to learn other details. They can use a field guide or an online resource for plant identification.

If the students identify plants in the field, leave it up to them to decide which part of the plant to collect; for example, they could collect the roots (for herbaceous plants only), stems, leaves, buds, or flowers. The students should estimate the amount of plant material needed to equal 5 g and then collect a little more. If the students do not identify each plant at the time it is collected, they will need to collect a specimen with at least 4–6 leaves on a stem from a tree or shrub; if collecting a herbaceous plant, they will need to pick the plant at ground level. Collecting plants in this fashion is necessary to be able to identify the plant later.

To save time and to ensure that there are both native and non-native plant species, you can collect the plants for the students and give them the plant identification and native status. Even if you do this, students can still choose which part of the plant to use in the investigation. Each species of plant should be stored in a refrigerator in a gallon-size sealed ziplock bag with two to four moist, thick paper towels until students are ready to use them.

Once the plants are identified and collected, additional class periods will be needed for plant extract and lettuce seed preparation, lettuce seed germination (2–3 days wait time), data collection, spreadsheet entry, statistical data analysis, and class comparisons. Students could work in pairs and perform three trials, with each pair having a different plant species, or the same plant could be assigned to three pairs of students and then the three sets of data could be combined to provide a better statistical analysis.

Procedure

1. Have the students tear about 5.0 g of each plant into tiny pieces (they can choose to use only leaves, stem, flowers, etc.) and place the plant pieces into a beaker with 100 ml of DI water. Tap water will work, but it adds another variable.
2. Have the students boil the plant and water mixture for about 15 minutes in the beaker on a hot plate. Smelling the brewed plant mixtures will often result in a set of distinct observations that should be recorded along with the developed color of the brewed plant solution. These observations are key to understanding that this brewing process is extracting and concentrating the organic and inorganic chemicals from the plant material.
3. The water should be evaporated until about 25 ml of liquid is left. The liquid will typically be brown, yellow, or green.
4. If students have boiled the mixture down to less than 25 ml of fluid, add DI water until the fluid reaches the 25 ml level of the beaker.
5. The students should allow the beakers to cool and then filter the plant material from the liquid through the cheesecloth into another clean beaker.
6. Tell the students to throw away the remaining solid plant material and keep the liquid plant extract. The extract should be cooled completely on a lab table.
7. For a typical investigation to assay the toxicity of the extracted plant material, you will need 6 petri dishes, 120 lettuce seeds, and 12 pieces of filter paper.
8. Have the students place one piece of filter paper on the bottom of each petri dish. If the paper is a little too big to fit, it should be pushed snugly down into the dish.
9. Have the students count out 20 lettuce seeds and place them into each dish, spacing the seeds as far apart as possible.
10. Have the students put another piece of filter paper on top of the seeds and press it down so it fits into the dish.
11. Repeat steps 8–10 for the other five dishes.
12. Have the students label three of the dishes "control" and the other three with the plant identity.
13. Have the students place about 4 ml of DI water into each control dish, or the amount needed to thoroughly saturate the filter paper without having standing water.
14. Have the students place about 4 ml of cooled extract into each extract dish, or the amount needed to thoroughly saturate the filter paper without having standing extract.

15. Have the students gather the control dishes and the extract dishes and place them in separate ziplock bags to reduce evaporation and cross-contamination.
16. Place the dishes in a darkened drawer and wait 2–3 days (or whatever the suggested germination period is).
17. Have the students check the seeds for sprouting (germination) and record the data on a spreadsheet for further analysis.
18. To check if the germination rates between the control and the extract sample are statistically different, have students perform a 2-PropZTest using a TI graphing calculator (see instructions later in the Teacher Information).
19. Have the students combine results trials into one data set and then perform a statistical analysis. If p is 0.05 or greater, the difference between the control and the sample is due to chance alone. If p is less than 0.05, there is a significant difference between the control and the sample.

Optional Extension: Serial Dilution of the Allelopathic Chemical to Determine the Toxic Concentration

To conduct this extension, you will need the following materials per group:

- 6 beakers or plastic cups
- 6 petri dishes
- 12 pieces of filter paper
- volumetric pipette
- plant extract

20. If the plant extract showed allelopathic effects on lettuce seed germination when compared with the control, perform a 10-fold serial dilution to determine the TC_{50} of the plant with the remaining extract. The TC_{50} is the toxic concentration at which 50% of the seeds do not germinate or are visibly affected. If some plant extracts did not show allelopathy, you can combine students into groups so that each group can perform one trial with an extract showing allelopathy.
21. Have the students label six beakers and six petri dishes as follows: control, 0.001%, 0.01%, 0.1%, 1%, and 10%.
22. Have the students prepare the petri dishes the same way they did in steps 8–10.
23. To prepare the serial dilutions, have the students put 9 ml of DI water into each beaker.
24. Consider the original extract the students "brewed" to represent the 100% concentration. Have the students take 1 ml of this and put it into the beaker labeled 10% and then mix well.
25. Now have the students take 1 ml of the solution from the 10% beaker and put it into the beaker labeled 1% and then mix well. Repeat this procedure for the remaining beakers (i.e., take 1 ml of solution from the 1% beaker and put it into the 0.1% beaker, take 1 ml of solution from the 0.1% beaker and put it

SCiLINKS. THE WORLD'S A CLICK AWAY
Topic: Allelopathy
Go to: *www.scilinks.org*
Code: WAT008

into the 0.01% beaker, and take 1 ml from the 0.01% beaker and put it into the 0.001% beaker.) The same pipette may be used throughout the dilution.

26. Have students repeat steps 12–17 and then interpret the data to find the TC_{50}.

Sample Data

Table 5.1. Sample Data for Lettuce Seed Germination After Exposure to Plant Extracts

Invasive Plant Name	Seeds Germinated				No. of Seeds Used	2-PropZTest for All Trials Combined	Significant Effect
	Trial 1	Trial 2	Trial 3	Total for All Trials			
Tree of heaven	3	0	0	3	60	3.0×10^{-20}	yes
Black alder	3	0	0	3	51	3.1×10^{-18}	yes
Bald cypress	1	5	0	6	61	3.3×10^{-18}	yes
Yellow sweet clover	1	0	0	1	57	3.1×10^{-21}	yes
Tartarian Honeysuckle	0	9	2	11	62	4.8×10^{-15}	yes
Garlic mustard	10	4	10	24	62	3.4×10^{-8}	yes
Common teasel	2	20	10	32	57	4.7×10^{-4}	yes
Milfoil	14	20	13	47	95	2.5×10^{-6}	yes
Purple loosestrife	12	12	14	38	77	5.7×10^{-6}	yes
Control	18	19	33	69	83		

For further examination of plant allelopathy, Table 5.2 shows the TC_{50} for one invasive (black alder) as determined from experimental data. In this case 0.001% is the TC_{50} because it is the percentage at which about half of the seeds are affected.

Table 5.2. Serial 10-Fold Dilution of Black Alder Extract

Dilution	No. of Seeds Used	No. of Seeds Germinated	% of Seeds Germinated	TC_{50}
10%	60	0	0	
1%	100	0	0	
0.1%	78	0	0	
0.01%	80	10	12.5	
0.001%	90	50	55	√
Control	65	50	77	

Other Optional Extensions

- Have students average the class results as a whole and compare toxicity between the varieties of plants to determine whether there is a difference between invasive and native plants.
- Have each student group analyze at least one of the same species and share results to make a more statistically significant test.
- Have the students measure the growth of the root tip as it emerges over a series of days. Many allelopathic plants simply slow the germination process rather than prevent it outright, and some species have evolved postgermination growth responses that increase how fast they grow to counteract their delayed germination. A fascinating extended study of evolutionary forces could result.

Instructions for Using the 2-PropZTest

1. Press the STAT key on the TI calculator.
2. Press the right arrow key until the TESTS tab is highlighted.
3. Select 2-PropZTest and press Enter.
4. The screen shown below will be displayed.

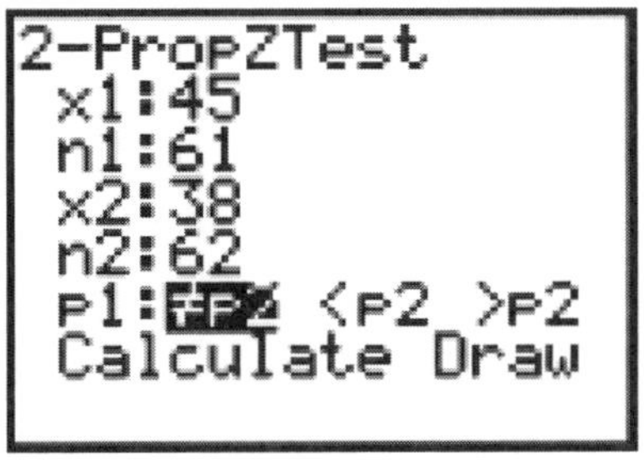

x1 = total seeds germinated for a specific plant solution
n1 = total seeds used for a specific plant solution
x2 = total seeds germinated for the control
n2 = total seeds used for the control

Make sure that " ≠ p2 " is selected, then press Calculate. The screen shown below will be displayed. The crucial value in this screen is the first *p* value. If this value is less than 0.05, then the difference between the plant solution germination and the control germination is statistically significant. If this value is 0.05 or greater, then the difference is *not* statistically significant.

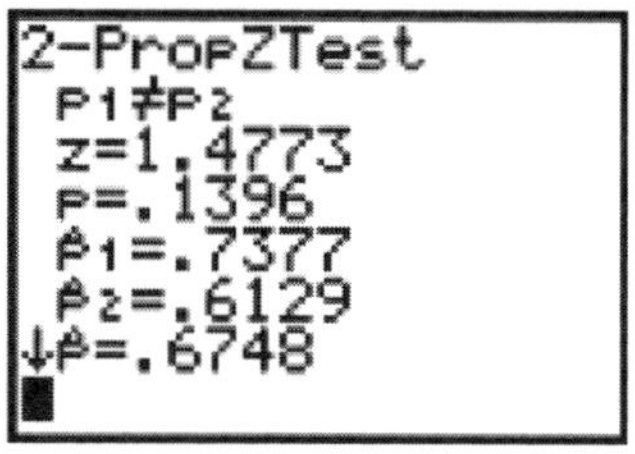

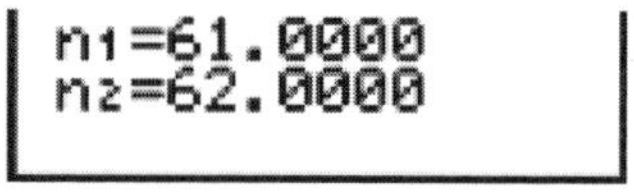

Answers to Questions in Student Handouts

1. Answers will vary.
2. Answers will vary, but there should not be a difference in the number of native and non-native plants that use allelochemicals. However, the use of allelochemicals may be one of the methods that non-native plants use to help them outcompete the native plants in the area. Therefore, those non-native plants that use allelochemicals and become aggressive invasive plants may be encountered more frequently.
3. Answers will vary, but the plants with the lowest percentage of germination will be the most toxic.

References

Ferguson, J. J., and B. Rathinasabapathi. July 2003. *Allelopathy: How plants suppress other plants.* Publication HS944. Gainesville: University of Florida, Institute of Food and Agricultural Sciences, Florida Cooperative Extension Service, Horticultural Sciences Department. *http://edis.ifas.ufl.edu/HS186*

Hart, S., M. Klepinger, H. Wandell, D. Garling, and L. Wolfson. 2000. *Integrated pest management for nuisance exotics in Michigan inland lakes.* Water Quality Series WQ-56. East Lansing: Michigan State University Extension. *www.deq.state.mi.us/documents/deq-water-great-lakes-aquatics-exotic4.pdf*

Ojala, T. 2001. Biological screening of plant coumarins. Academic dissertation, University of Helsinki. *http://ethesis.helsinki.fi/julkaisut/mat/farma/vk/ojala/biologic.pdf*

Oudhia, P. *Parthenium hysterophorus:* Traditional medicinal uses. *www.hort.purdue.edu/newcrop/CropFactSheets/parthenium.html*

Ramey, V. 2005. Plant management in Florida waters. *http://aquat1.ifas.ufl.edu/guide/invplant.html*

Rivenshield, A. 2006. Allelopathy. Ithaca, NY: Cornell University. *http://csip.cornell.edu/Projects/CEIRP/AR/Allelopathy.htm*

Measuring Plant Allelopathy

Student Handout A

In this investigation, you will select, identify, and test a common plant for allelopathy by extracting the plant's natural chemicals and measuring the effect on the germination of lettuce seeds. You will analyze the data statistically to determine if the germination of seeds exposed to plant extract differs significantly from the germination of seeds in the control condition.

Objective

To compare the allelopathic effects of native and non-native plants on the germination of seeds.

Materials Needed Per Group

- a native plant and a non-native plant (stored in ziplock bags until ready for use)
- 6 petri dishes
- moistened paper towels
- 12 pieces of size 3 filter paper or paper towels cut to fit a petri dish
- 120 lettuce seeds (Any seed that germinates in 2–3 days is fine. Seeds are available in the plant and garden section of the supermarket. It is advisable not to use old seed packages because the percentage that germinates will be lower.)
- hot plate (to be shared as needed)
- 2 beakers
- 1 100 ml graduated cylinder
- 1 10 ml graduated cylinder
- 1 6"× 6" piece of cheesecloth
- deionized (DI) water, or any type of purified water
- Texas Instruments (TI) graphing calculator
- gloves (optional)

Procedure

1. Tear about 5.0 g of the plant into tiny pieces (leaves and stem) and place the plant pieces into a beaker with 100 ml of DI water.
2. Boil the plant and water mixture for about 15 minutes in the beaker on a hot plate. Smelling the brewed plant mixtures will often result in a set of distinct observations that should be recorded along with the developed color of the brewed plant solution.
3. The water should be evaporated until about 25 ml of liquid is left. The liquid will typically be brown, yellow, or green.

4. If the mixture has been boiled down to less than 25 ml of fluid, add DI water until 25 ml is reached.
5. Allow the beakers to cool and then filter the plant material from the liquid through the cheesecloth into another clean beaker.
6. Throw away the remaining solid plant material and keep the liquid plant extract. Cool it completely on a lab table.
7. Take 6 petri dishes, 120 lettuce seeds, and 12 pieces of filter paper.
8. Place one piece of filter paper on the bottom of each petri dish. If the paper is a little too big to fit, push it snugly down into the dish.
9. Count out 20 lettuce seeds and place them into the dish, spacing them as far apart as possible.
10. Put another piece of filter paper on top of the seeds and press it down so it fits into the dish.
11. Repeat steps 8–10 for the other five dishes.
12. Label three of the dishes "control" and the other three with your plant identity.
13. Place about 4 ml of DI water into each control dish, or the amount needed to thoroughly saturate the filter paper without having standing water.
14. Place about 4 ml of cooled extract into each extract dish, or the amount needed to thoroughly saturate the filter paper without having standing extract.
15. Gather the control dishes and the extract dishes and place them in separate Ziplock bags to reduce evaporation and cross-contamination.
16. Place the dishes in a darkened drawer and wait 2-3 days (or whatever the suggested germination period is for your seeds).
17. Check seeds for sprouting (germination) and record the data on the table in your answer sheet for further analysis.
18. To check if the germination rates between the control and the extract sample are statistically different, perform a 2-PropZTest on a TI graphing calculator. See the teacher for instructions if you do not know how to perform this test.
19. Combine trials into one data set and then perform a statistical analysis. If p is 0.05 or greater, the difference between the control and the sample is due to chance alone. If p is less than 0.05, there is a significant difference between the control and the sample. Record in your data table whether or not there is a significant difference between your sample and the control.

Optional Extension

To perform this extension, you will need the following materials:

- 6 beakers or plastic cups
- 6 petri dishes
- 12 pieces of filter paper
- volumetric pipette
- plant extract

20. If the plant showed allelopathic effects on lettuce seed germination when compared with the control, perform a 10-fold serial dilution to determine the TC_{50} of the plant with the remaining extract.
21. Label six beakers and six petri dishes as follows: control, 0.001%, 0.01%, 0.1%, 1%, and 10%.
22. Prepare the petri dishes the same way you did in steps 8–10.
23. To prepare the serial dilutions, put 9 ml of DI water into each beaker.
24. You will be starting with the extract you "brewed," which represents the 100% concentration. Take 1 ml of this and put it into the beaker labeled 10%. Mix well.
25. Now take 1 ml of the solution from the 10% beaker and put it into the beaker labeled 1%, and mix well. Repeat this procedure for the remaining beakers: take 1 ml of solution from the 1% beaker and put it into the 0.1% beaker, take 1 ml of solution from the 0.1% beaker and put it into the 0.01% beaker, and take 1 ml from the 0.01% beaker and put it into the 0.001% beaker. The same pipette may be used throughout the dilution.
26. Set up your new petri dishes with seeds and serial dilutions of extract the same way you did before (steps 12–16).
27. Check the seeds for sprouting, create a spreadsheet, and record the germination data.
28. Calculate the percentage of seeds germinated to find the TC_{50}.

Name______________________________

Questions on Plant Allelopathy

Name	Seeds Germinated				No. of Seeds Used	2-PropZTest for All Trials Combined	Significant Effect
	Trial 1	Trial 2	Trial 3	Total for All Trials			

1. Did your plant produce an allelochemical that affected lettuce seed germination? Explain how you know this from your observations and your data.

2. List all your classmates' plants that showed an effect on lettuce seed germination. Identify which plants are invasive and which are native. Is there any difference between native and non-native plants in the frequency of allelopathy?

3. If the class conducted serial dilutions, which plant seemed to be the most toxic? Explain how you came to this conclusion.

Measuring Plant Allelopathy

Student Handout B

Objective

To compare the allelopathic effects of native and non-native plants on the germination of seeds.

In this lab investigation, you will select, identify, and test a common plant for allelopathy by extracting the plant's natural chemicals and measuring the effect on the germination of lettuce seeds. You will analyze the data statistically to determine if the germination of seeds exposed to plant extract differs significantly from the germination of seeds in the control condition. If the plant shows an allelopathic effect, then the TC_{50} will be determined.

The first step in designing this lab investigation is to make a hypothesis. The following is an example of a hypothesis: *My invasive plant does not show allelopathic phenomena because there were different plants growing around it in the environment in which it lived.*

State your hypothesis.

____

____

____

How will you test this hypothesis using the materials and methods listed below? Think about the following questions:

1. What types of data should be collected to test your hypothesis?
2. What should your controls be?
3. How many trials should there be?
4. How many seeds should be used in each trial?
5. For how long should the experiment be carried out?
6. How can effects like evaporation be reduced so that the seeds remain moist?

Write down a step-by-step procedure, and create a data table for the results. Set up the experiment after the teacher has approved the procedure. Begin boiling the plants first, because the mixture will take time to cool. While boiling and cooling, set up the rest of the experiment. When data collection is complete, enter the data into a spreadsheet and answer the questions at the end of this handout. Turn in the hypothesis, the written procedure, the data table spreadsheet, and the answers to the questions at the end of this Student Handout.

Materials

- a native and a non-native plant (stored in ziplock bags until ready for use)
- petri dishes
- hot plate
- moistened paper towels
- size 3 filter paper or paper towels cut to fit a petri dish
- lettuce seeds (Any seed that germinates in 2–3 days is fine.)
- beakers or plastic cups
- 10 ml graduated cylinders
- deionized (DI) water, or any type of purified water
- Texas Instruments (TI) graphing calculator

Methods

Extraction of Allelochemicals

Extract allelochemicals from plant material by boiling them. Tear about 5.0 g of plant leaves and stem into small pieces and put the pieces into a beaker with 100 ml of DI water. Boil the mixture for about 15 minutes in a beaker on a hot plate. If the solution has evaporated to less than 25 ml, add DI water until 25 ml is reached. Strain the extract through cheesecloth and dispose of the solid plant material. Allow the plant extracts to cool on the lab bench before using them.

Statistical Analysis

To determine if the germination rates between the control and the sample are statistically different, use the 2-PropZTest on a Texas Instruments graphing calculator (if you need further instructions, see your teacher). Combine trials into one data set and then perform 2-PropZTest statistical analysis. If p is 0.05 or greater, the difference between the control and the sample is due to chance alone. If p is less than 0.05, there is a significant difference between the control and the sample. Record in your data table whether or not there is a significant difference between your sample and the control.

10-Fold Serial Dilutions to Determine TC_{50}

Starting with the extract "brewed," which represents the 100% concentration, take 1 ml of this 100% concentration and put it into a beaker labeled 10%, add 9 ml of water, and mix well. Now take 1 ml of the solution from your 10% beaker and put it into a beaker labeled 1%, add 9 ml of water, and mix well. Continue until you have reached your desired concentration. As long as the dilutions are in order from a greater concentration to a lower concentration, the same pipette may be used throughout the dilution.

Name______________________________

Questions on Plant Allelopathy

1. Did your plant produce an allelochemical that affected lettuce seed germination? Explain how you know this from your observations and your data.

2. List all your classmates' plants that showed an effect on lettuce seed germination. Identify which plants are invasive and which are native. Is there any difference between native and non-native plants in the frequency of allelopathy?

3. Determine the TC_{50} from your serial dilution. Which plant appears to be the most toxic in the class?

CHAPTER 6

Stream Channel Morphology

Teacher Information

Background

Historically, streams and rivers were the major transportation routes for people and goods in this country. Many large cities, such as Chicago, Detroit, and Grand Rapids (Michigan), were built next to waterways because the easiest and most efficient means of transporting goods was via the river to the Great Lakes.

With farming and urban development of watersheds, our streams and waterways began to change. For example, in Holland, Michigan, the Ottawa Indians, who used the area for summer hunting grounds long before the Europeans arrived in 1849, noted that streams were being dammed up and polluted when they left the area in 1850. As part of this early development, the land was cleared of trees, which resulted in streams being warmed as the shade canopy was removed. To use this new source of lumber, sawmills became commonplace. The sawdust from sawmills and erosion due to loss of vegetation filled in the streams, making them more shallow, warmer, and more turbid. In addition to erosion, the clearing of the land also increased runoff, which in time lowered the base flow of the waterways (Van Koevering 1960).

As development continued, people manipulated streams by changing their channel *morphology* (shape). Straight stream channels transport water and sediment faster, whereas meandering streams slow the flow of water. When land was being settled in this country, it was a common practice to straighten stream channels and make new ones to drain the land more efficiently.

When humans change the natural topography, certain effects are likely to be seen in a watershed. The transportation of water and sediment increases when streams are straightened and, with the increased flow rate of water, erosion also increases. All of these factors increase turbidity and can have a negative effect on the waterways and most lakes. A degraded visual appearance will be the most noticeable effect, but animal and plant life will also begin to change as streams are changed.

Objective

To compare how channel morphology affects the flow of water and the transportation of sediment.

Materials Needed Per Group

- 100 g of sand
- waste container to catch effluent, with an opening 30 cm wide
- electronic balance (students may share at each lab table)
- 50 ml graduated cylinder
- stopwatch
- Styrofoam stream table (You can buy Styrofoam at any home improvement store. See instructions below for making the stream table.)
- aluminum foil

Instructions for Making Styrofoam Stream Tables

Styrofoam boards can be used as an inexpensive alternative to commercial stream tables. Their construction is very simple, although quite messy. First cut 3 in. thick (or thicker) Styrofoam into 1 ft. × 3 ft. sections; these sections are the stream boards. The channels that will be cut into the stream boards can be traced onto the foam first. You will need to cut two channels on each side of the stream board, using a standard router with a ½ in. bit. Since a router is designed to carve wood, it very rapidly cuts channels in the Styrofoam, like a warm knife through butter. It takes just a few minutes per board to do this. Be sure to do this fabrication in an area where you can clean up the millions of small Styrofoam particles that will be created in the milling process, and allow time to clean up afterward.

At the top of each channel, use the router to make a space for students to pour water at the top of the stream. On one side of the Styrofoam board, router out a straight channel and a meandering channel. (Meandering channels should have at least four bends.) On the other side of the board, router out the straight and meandering channels again but put three depressions in each channel approximately equal distances apart to act as sediment catch basins. Figure 6.1 shows an example of a Styrofoam stream board.

Figure 6.1. Styrofoam Stream Board With Straight and Meandering Channels

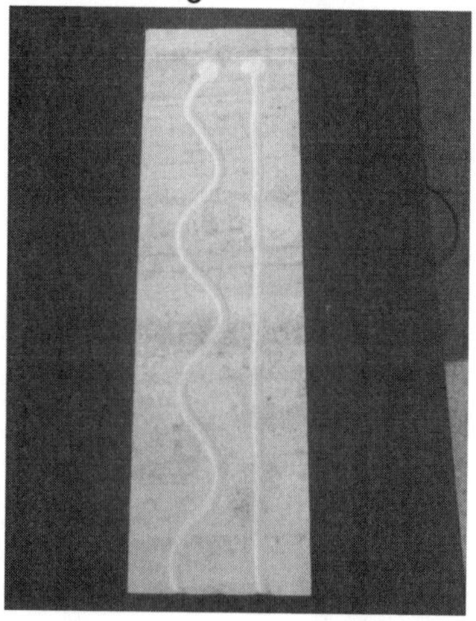

Suggested Class Preparation and Format

Although construction of the Styrofoam stream boards will take a few hours outside of class, the boards can typically be reused for several years. Lab setup time in class is minimal. This investigation could be used in an earth science course when studying hydrology or in a biology course when studying the effects of erosion. It could also be used in any science class in its inquiry form to present the students with the opportunity to design a relatively easy experiment.

You may give students a traditional set of instructions (Student Handout A) or use a more open-ended exploratory investigation, in which only the methods are explained and students must design their own set of experiments and methods (Student Handout B). The investigation can be done in two 50-minute class periods using the three-part procedure outlined here and in Student Handout A, with the experiment taking place in the first lab period and analysis of class data and calculations conducted in a second class period. You can have the students work in pairs, with each completing one trial, and then combine the class data to obtain an average. (Having each student pair complete three trials of each laboratory section is too cumbersome.) If the investigation is run using the inquiry approach (see Student Handout B), students will need an additional class period to do research and design their lab. This is a great experiment for students to design on their own because it is simple enough that they will not get overwhelmed. Students will come up with different designs than the one suggested here, so you need to be flexible.

After class data have been examined, you can discuss the advantages and disadvantages of each type of stream channel and the impact they have on a watershed.

One flaw in this experiment is that the stream tables do not allow you to see sediment that is eroded from the stream bank.

The three-part procedure is described in the next section. Each part can be performed independently of the others.

Student Procedure

Part I: Determine Placement of Deposition in Stream Channels

1. Place the Styrofoam stream board at a 30-degree angle on the lab table.
2. Position a waste container under the stream channel outlet to catch any effluent.
3. Weigh 10 g of sand and pour it into the top quarter of the straight channel.
4. Measure 25 ml of water and pour it into the straight channel at a steady rate.
5. Draw a diagram of where the sand was deposited in the channel.
6. Repeat steps 2–5 with the meandering channel.
7. You may need to redo this until you see a pattern of sedimentation. Be sure to rinse out any residual sand between measurements.

Part II: Determine the Rate of Flow in Stream Channels

1. Place the Styrofoam stream board at a 30-degree angle (low gradient) on the lab table.
2. Position a waste container under the stream channel outlet to catch any effluent.
3. Measure 25 ml of water and pour it into the straight channel at a steady rate.
4. As pouring begins, start the stopwatch; stop it when the water first reaches the bottom of the stream. This may have to be practiced a few times to get an accurate result.
5. Record all data, enter the data on a spreadsheet, and calculate the average time for the class.

Part III: Determine the Amount of Sediment Transported in Stream Channels

1. Using the Styrofoam stream board with the depression side up, position the board at a 30-degree angle.
2. Position a waster container below the outlet to catch any effluent.
3. Get a piece of aluminum foil that is about the size of a sheet of paper and cut out 2 cm × 7 cm rectangles. Fold the rectangles in half and place them within the depressions in both stream channels. [Teacher Note: The students will need 12 rectangles total, if they will be performing this twice using the two different gradients as suggested in the optional extension.]
4. Using your finger, mold each aluminum foil rectangle to fit each depression; cut off any excess.
5. Using a Sharpie marker, label the depressions of the straight channel on the back of each aluminum foil cup, as follows: ST (top), SM (middle), and SB (bottom); then mark the depressions of the meandering channel as MT, MM, and MB.
6. Using the electronic balance, weigh each aluminum cup and record the mass on a spreadsheet.
7. Weigh 10 g of sand.
8. Measure 25 ml of water.
9. Pour the 10 g of sand in the straight channel between the top and the first depression.
10. Place the aluminum cups in their proper depressions.
11. Pour 25 ml of water down the straight channel, again making sure all the water flows into the channel. Pour at a steady rate. Note any sediment coming out of the bottom of the stream.
12. Very carefully remove the aluminum cups and set them on a piece of paper towel on the lab counter. The paper towel should be labeled in advance with the same abbreviations listed in step 5.

13. Repeat this procedure (steps 6–12) for the meandering channel.
14. Let the aluminum foil cups dry over night. [Teacher Note: As a quicker alternative, the cups could be set on a hot plate for about 20 minutes to dry.]
15. Weigh the aluminum cups with the sand, and subtract the initial mass of the aluminum foil to find the mass of the sand deposited in each location. Record the data on a spreadsheet.

Optional Extensions

- All three procedures can be repeated using a gradient of 60 degrees to demonstrate the role of topography in flow rate and sediment deposition.
- For Part II of the investigation, velocity could be calculated and graphed instead of only time being recorded as indicated in the procedure.

Sample Data

Figure 6.2 provides sample data for channel morphology versus time of water travel. Note that the water in the straight channel gets to the bottom of the board almost twice as fast as the water in the meandering channel.

Figure 6.2. Sample Data for Channel Morphology Versus Time of Water Travel

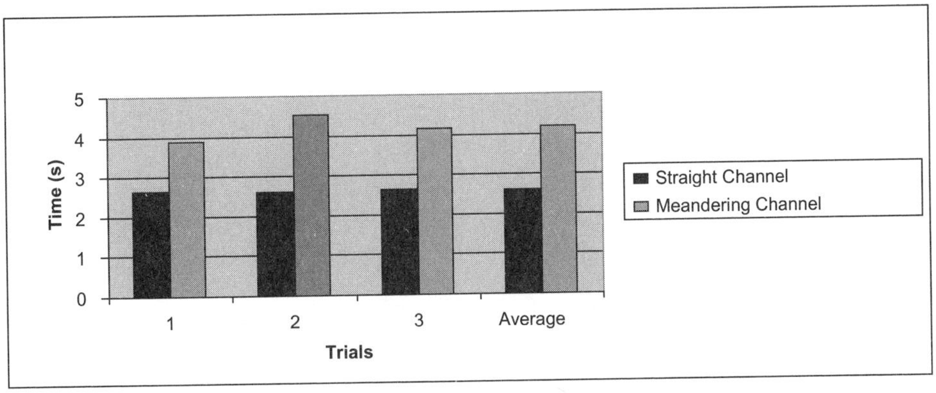

Figure 6.3 and 6.4 illustrate the amount of sediment dispersed in straight and meandering channels over four trials—two with the stream table at a gradient of 30 degrees and two with the stream table at a gradient of 60 degrees. In the low-gradient trials, the sediment is dispersed throughout the straight channel but stays at the top of the meandering channel. In the high-gradient trials, the sediment is again dispersed throughout the straight channel but because of the higher gradient is transported farther down the channel. In the meandering channel, sediment is not transported as far as in the straight channel but is transported farther at the high gradient then at the low gradient.

Figure 6.3. Amount of Sediment in Straight and Meandering Channels at Low Gradient (30°)

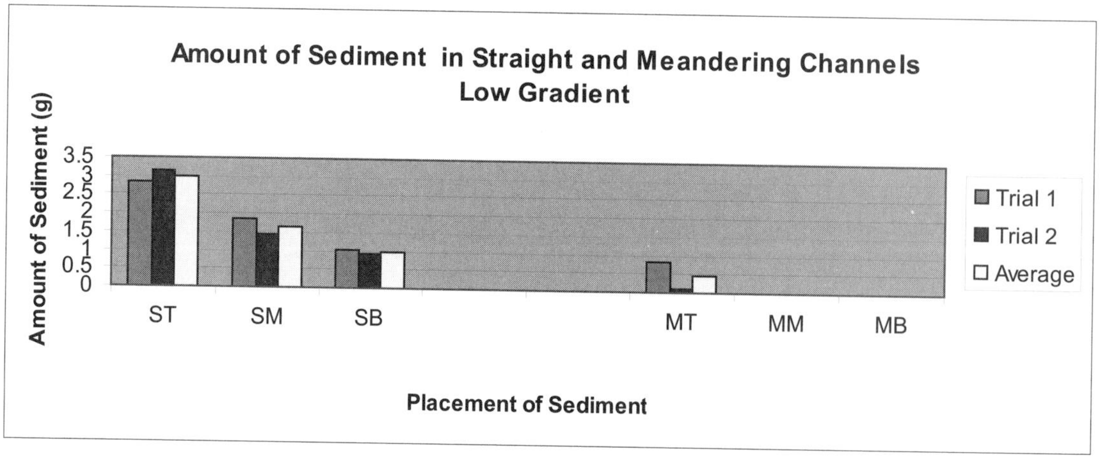

Figure 6.4. Amount of Sediment in Straight and Meandering Channels at High Gradient (60°)

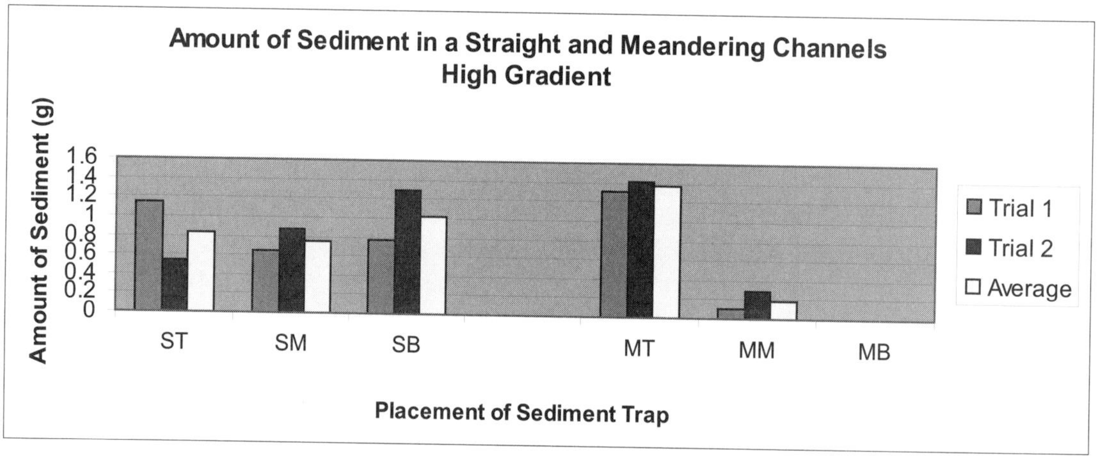

Key to Figures 6.3 and 6.4

ST = straight channel top
SM = straight channel middle
SB = straight channel bottom
MT = meandering channel top
MM = meandering channel middle
MB = meandering channel bottom

SCILINKS
THE WORLD'S A CLICK AWAY

Topic: Stream Deposits
Go to: *www.scilinks.org*
Code: WAT009

Answers to Questions in Student Handouts

1. Diagrams will vary but should show sediment deposition in the middle in a straight channel and on the inner bends in a meandering channel.
2. Straight channels will get rid of excess water faster but also will transport sediments faster. Meandering channels slow the flow of water and let sediments settle out. Since phosphorus is attached to the sediments, meandering channels are better at slowing its transportation. Students might cite their times of water travel, deposition patterns, or sediment amounts that were transported to support their answer.
3. In this lab students should see meandering channels experience more erosion than straight channels because of the high velocity of water on the outer banks, but sediment will have time to settle out and be deposited on the inner banks due to lower flow rates. Straight channels have the fastest flow of water in the middle of the channel and therefore experience less erosion, because the fastest flowing water is not touching the banks as it is in the meandering channel. However, in nature, erosion depends on flow rate. In general, erosion might be significantly less in a meandering stream if it has a slower flow of water, whereas erosion could be greater in the straight stream because of the higher velocity of water. In some cases, a meandering stream may experience more erosion because meandering streams tend erode themselves as a result of the high erosion rates on the outside of their meanders. The degree of erosion depends on gradient, channel width and depth, and bottom roughness, all of which affect the flow rate and hence the erosion rate.

Reference

Van Koevering, A. 1960. *Legends of the Dutch.* Zeeland, MI: Zeeland Record Company.

Stream Channel Morphology Lab

Student Handout A

Background

In this investigation, the effects of stream channel morphology, which is the shape of the stream, will be examined in relation to rate of water flow and the transport of sediments. In addition, the topography, or surface contours, of a stream will be examined to see how it affects the time of water travel.

Objective

To compare how channel morphology affects the flow of water and the transportation of sediment.

Materials Needed Per Group

- 100 g of sand
- waste container to catch effluent
- electronic balance (to be shared at each lab table)
- 50 ml graduated cylinder
- stopwatch
- Styrofoam stream table
- aluminum foil

Procedure

Part I: Determine Placement of Deposition in Stream Channels

1. Place the Styrofoam stream board at a 30-degree angle on the lab table.
2. Position a waste container under the stream channel outlet to catch any effluent.
3. Weigh 10 g of sand and pour into the top quarter of the straight channel.
4. Measure 25 ml of water and pour it into the straight channel at a steady rate.
5. Draw a diagram of where the sand was deposited in the channel.
6. Repeat steps 2–5 with the meandering channel.
7. You may need to redo this until you see a pattern of sedimentation. Be sure to rinse out any residual sand between measurements.

Part II: Determine the Rate of Flow in Stream Channels

1. Place the Styrofoam stream board at a 30-degree angle (low gradient) on the lab table.
2. Position a waste container under the stream channel outlet to catch any effluent.
3. Measure 25 ml of water and pour it into the straight channel at a steady rate.

4. As pouring begins, start the stopwatch; stop it when the water first reaches the bottom of the stream. This may have to be practiced a few times to get an accurate result.
5. Record all data, enter the data on a spreadsheet, and calculate the average time for the class.
6. If instructed to do so by your teacher, position the stream board at a 60-degree angle (high gradient) on the lab table.
7. Repeat steps 2–5.

Part III: Determine the Amount of Sediment Transported in Stream Channels

1. Using the Styrofoam stream board with the depression side up, position the board at a 30-degree angle.
2. Position a waste container below the outlet to catch any effluent.
3. Get a piece of aluminum foil that is about the size of a sheet of paper and cut out 2 cm × 7 cm rectangles. Fold the rectangles in half and place them within the depressions in both stream channels. You will need 12 rectangles for each trial, if you will be performing this measurement twice using two different gradients.
4. Using your finger, mold each aluminum foil rectangle to fit each depression; cut off any excess.
5. Using a Sharpie marker, label the depressions of the straight channel on the back of each aluminum foil cup, as follows: ST (top), SM (middle), and SB (bottom); then mark the depressions of the meandering channel as MT, MM, and MB.
6. Using the electronic balance, weigh each aluminum cup and record the mass on the spreadsheet.
7. Weigh 10 g of sand.
8. Measure 25 ml of water.
9. Pour the 10 g of sand in the straight channel between the top and the first depression.
10. Place aluminum cups in their proper depressions.
11. Pour 25 ml of water down the channel, again making sure all the water flows into the channel. Pour at a steady rate. Note any sediment coming out of the bottom of the stream.
12. Very carefully remove the aluminum cups and set them on a piece of paper towel on the lab counter. The paper towel should be labeled in advance with the same abbreviations listed in step 5.
13. Repeat this procedure (steps 6–12) for the meandering channel. If instructed to do so by your teacher, repeat the procedure at the high gradient for the straight and meandering channels.
14. Let the aluminum foil cups dry overnight.
15. Weigh the aluminum cups with the sand and subtract the initial mass of the aluminum foil to find the mass of the sand deposited in each location. Record the data on a spreadsheet.

Name________________________________

Questions on Stream Channel Morphology

Part I

1. Draw a diagram of a straight and a meandering stream channel; sketch where sediment was deposited.

Part II

Table 1. Channel Morphology Versus Time of Water for Low Gradient

Time (s)	
Straight Channel	Meandering Channel
Class Average	

Part III

Table 2. Amount of Sediment Deposited Using a Low Gradient

Position and Stream Channel	Mass of Aluminum Cup (g)	Mass of Aluminum and Sand (g)	Mass of Sand (g)	Observations
ST				
SM				
SB				
MT				
MM				
MB				
Class Average				

When data collection is complete, make bar graphs for Parts II and III and answer the following questions:

2. Would a straight channel or a meandering channel be better for slowing the transportation of phosphorus within a watershed? Support your answer with at least two pieces of evidence from your lab data.

   ____

   ____

   ____

   ____

3. Which type of stream channel will experience the most erosion? Use specific evidence from your experiment to support your answer.

   ____

   ____

   ____

   ____

Stream Channel Morphology Lab

Student Handout B

Objective

To compare how channel morphology affects the flow of water and the transportation of sediment.

In this investigation, the effects of stream channel morphology will be examined in relation to rate of water flow and the transport of sediments. Many streams in the United States have been hydrologically modified as a result of development. When changing the natural topography of a stream channel, certain effects are likely to be seen in a watershed. The transportation of water and sediment increases when streams are straightened and, with the increased flow rate of water, erosion also increases. All of these factors increase turbidity and can have a negative effect on the waterways and most lakes. A degraded visual appearance will be the most noticeable effect, but animal and plant life will also begin to change as streams are changed.

The first step in designing this investigation is to make a hypothesis. An example of a hypothesis is as follows: *Straight streams flow faster and transport more sediments than do meandering streams.*

State your hypothesis.

____

____

____

____

How will you test this hypothesis using the materials and methods listed below? Think about the following questions:

1. What types of data should be collected to test your hypothesis?
2. What should your controls be?
3. How many trials should there be?
4. How much sand and water should be used?
5. How will sand and wastewater be collected to ensure it does not go down the drains?
6. How will the effects of topography be tested?

Write down a step-by-step procedure and prepare a data table for the results. Set up the experiment after the teacher has approved your procedure. When data collection is complete, enter the data into a spreadsheet, prepare bar graphs, and answer the questions at the end of this Student Handout.

Materials

- 100 g of sand
- waste container to catch effluent
- electronic balance (to be shared at each lab table)
- 50 ml graduated cylinder
- stopwatch
- Styrofoam stream table
- aluminum foil

Method for Collecting Sediment in Stream Channel Traps

Depressions have been made into the stream channels on one side of the stream board. Only use this side when you want to collect sediments. To collect sediments, get a piece of aluminum foil that is about the size of a sheet of paper and cut out 2 cm × 7 cm rectangles. Fold the rectangles in half and place them within the depression in both stream channels. Using your finger, mold each aluminum foil rectangle to fit each depression; cut off any excess. Using a Sharpie marker, label the depressions of the straight channel on the back of each aluminum foil cup, as follows: ST (top), SM (middle), and SB (bottom); then mark the depressions of the meandering channel as MT, MM, and MB. Weigh aluminum cups and record the data on a spreadsheet. Run the experiment. Let the sand-filled aluminum cups dry overnight, then weigh them the following day to determine the mass of the sand transported down the stream channel.

Name_______________________________

Questions on Stream Channel Morphology

1. Draw a diagram of a straight and meandering stream channel; sketch where sediment was deposited.

2. Would a straight channel or a meandering channel be better for slowing the transportation of phosphorus? Support your answer with at least two pieces of evidence from your lab data.

____

____

____

____

3. Which type of stream channel will experience the most erosion? Use specific evidence from your experiment to support your answer.

____

____

____

____

CHAPTER 7

Calculating Stream Discharge

Teacher Information*

Background

Streamflow, or discharge, is defined by the U.S. Geological Survey (USGS) as the volume of water flowing past a fixed point in a fixed unit of time. Stream discharge is measured in cubic feet per second or cubic meters per second. The discharge of a stream can be affected by many things, including topography and channel morphology. However, rainfall (the more rainfall there is, the greater the discharge) and land use have the greatest effect on stream discharge. Lack of vegetation increases surface runoff, whereas the presence of vegetation slows runoff. Areas that have no vegetation but are pervious are better at decreasing runoff than impervious areas because the rain can infiltrate the ground. Rain that falls on impervious surfaces (pavement, rooftops, etc.) rapidly runs off into the waterways, and this may cause flash flooding.

Being able to calculate stream discharge is important because this information is needed to make flood frequency predictions.

Objective

To measure the discharge of a stream.

Materials Needed Per Group

- area with stream access
- 3 pairs of waders
- metric tape measure (at least 50 m)
- meter stick
- Vernier flow rate meter (see instructions below) with operating system of choice (e.g., LabPro, GoLink)
- 6 V lantern battery

*The idea and lab information for this investigation were based on Mark Luttenton's Aquatic Methods class at Grand Valley State University, Allendale, Michigan.

Methods

Using the Vernier Flow Rate Meter

The Vernier flow rate meter is an inexpensive option for calculating flow rate. These items can be purchased directly from Vernier (*www.vernier.com*) or a science supply company. Refer to the user's manual for meter preparation and long-term care. A 6 V lantern battery should be used in the field to power the Vernier equipment. Vernier sells the necessary connecting cable.

Calculating Total Discharge of a Stream

The area of each cell in the stream can be calculated in the same way as the area of a trapezoid.

$$\text{Area} = \frac{(side + side)}{2}(width)$$

where the width is the width of each cell, which is 0.5 m or 1 m (this is the distance between depth readings), and the sides are the sides of each cell, which are the depth readings.

After finding the area for each cell, calculate the discharge for each cell:

$$\text{Discharge} = (area)\,(flow\ rate)$$

Find the total discharge for the stream by adding individual cell discharges together. If depth was measured in centimeters, convert it to meters when calculating the area.

Suggested Class Preparation and Format

This investigation could be used when studying the effects of erosion in an earth science class. The flow rate of the stream is directly related to the amount of sediment that travels downstream. This investigation also fits in well with the stream channel morphology investigation in Chapter 6 and the flood frequency analysis investigation in Chapter 8 of this book. It is a nice break from traditional indoor laboratory work and allows students to be outside in the field and to actually see what they have been learning in class.

Time spent learning how to use equipment will be minimal. This investigation is a field exercise, so you will need access to a stream and transportation to get there. Actual setup involves only setting out equipment for students to access.

Two 50-minute class periods will be needed to complete this investigation. In the first period you will teach students how to calculate discharge and how to use equipment; the second period will be in the field collecting data. Students can be assigned calculations for homework.

When conducting a field exercise with students, it is important that each person have something to do so that everyone stays on task. Keeping all students on task is especially hard with this activity because only five students can collect data at a time. You will need two students to hold the tape measure across the stream, one student to measure stream depth, one student to hold the flow rate meter, and one student to hold the LabPro (or other device that you selected). The rest of the class should be directed to sit on the banks and record data. They can also work on data calculations while they wait, to decrease homework time. Another possibility would be to couple this field exercise with others in this book (e.g., collecting sediments for comparison of phosphorus levels or collecting macroinvertebrate samples) so that all students have something hands-on to do. If students will be performing other investigations at the same time, they will need to stay downstream of the students collecting the stream discharge data.

Procedure

1. Have students select a section of the stream that does not have any debris, ripples, or meanders directly upstream from the site to be measured.
2. Have a student stand in the stream at the bank holding one end of the tape measure, and have a second student walk across the stream holding the other end of the tape measure. They should hold the tape measure tightly above the stream surface and keep it in this position the entire time. This step is necessary to know where to take depth and flow rate measurements.
3. Once the tape measure is set up across the stream, select a third student to measure the stream depth in meters every 0.5 m or 1.0 m, depending on the width of the stream (use 0.5 cm for smaller streams). Students can read off the depth in centimeters if they find this easier, but the measurements will need to be converted to meters when recording the data.
4. While stream depth is being measured, two other students can begin measuring the flow rate. The propeller should be placed into the water in the middle of the water column; it should not be placed directly on the bottom or the top of the stream. The flow rate meter should be positioned in between the 0.5 m depth readings so that the first flow rate will be collected at 0.25 m across the stream, the second at 0.75 m, and so on at intervals of 0.5 m.
5. Have the students record the data in a cross-sectional diagram of the stream.
6. Have the students calculate the total discharge of the stream.

Sample Data

The stream is divided into cells every 0.5 m. The depth of the cell is measured at both banks and at the boundaries of each cell. The flow rate is measured in the middle of each cell. Students can draw a diagram like the one in Figure 7.1 to represent the stream and then record depths on the banks and vertically along the dotted lines and flow rates horizontally along the top. A diagram to record data is suggested instead of a table because it gives a better visual representation. Students may get confused when performing their calculations if the data are in tabular format.

Figure 7.1. Cross Section of a Stream

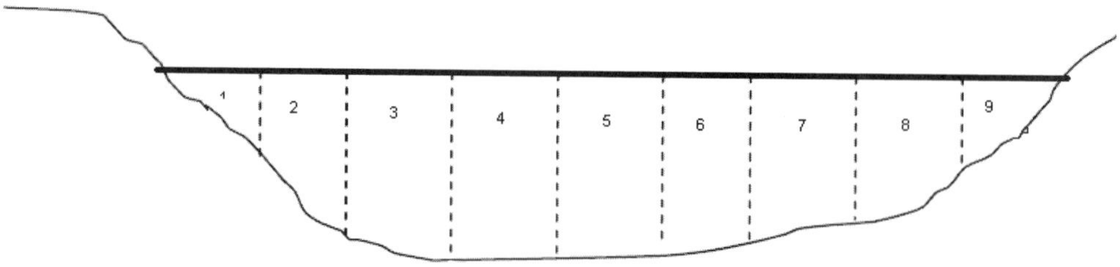

A sample calculation for one cell is shown below:

$$\text{Area} = \frac{(0\text{ m} + 2\text{ m})}{2}(0.5\text{ m})$$

$$= 0.5\text{ m}^2$$

$$\text{Discharge} = (0.5\text{ m}^2)(0.001\text{ m/s})$$

$$= 0.0005\text{ m}^3/\text{s}$$

Table 7.1 contains sample data with calculations. As another option for calculations, students can use a spreadsheet and create the formulas needed.

Table 7.1. Sample Data for Calculating Stream Discharge

Cell	Depth (m)	Flow Rate (m/s)	Area of a Trapezoid (m^2)	Discharge (m^3/s)
	0			
1	2	0.001	0.5	0.0005
2	2.5	0.001	1.125	0.001125
3	3	0.02	1.375	0.0275
4	3	0.1	1.5	0.15
5	2.75	0.03	1.4375	0.043125
6	2.25	0.02	1.25	0.025
7	2	0.01	1.0625	0.010625
8	1.5	0.01	0.875	0.00875
9	0	0.001	0.375	0.000375
			Total Discharge:	**0.266625**

Optional Extension

If possible, pick a location where two streams come together. Students can measure the discharge of each stream upstream of where the streams join and then downstream of their juncture. Once students have calculated the total discharge for each stream, they can add together their two upstream values to see if the total equals their downstream value. This option will involve more students in the hands-on activity and keep them on task.

Answers to Questions 1 and 2 in Student Handout

1. It is important to monitor stream discharge to be able to make hydrographs and predict flood frequency and the amount of sediments being transported.
2. Hydrograph A represents a more urbanized watershed because of the spike in flow. An urbanized watershed contains a lot of impervious surfaces, so runoff does not infiltrate into the ground but runs very rapidly into waterways, causing big increases in stream discharge in a matter of minutes or hours. Hydrograph B represents a nonurbanized watershed, which has more pervious surfaces. In this type of watershed, rain can infiltrate into the ground and be absorbed by vegetation and soils and then into groundwater. This process can take up to 2–3 days, and the volume of water entering the waterways is not nearly as much.

Reference

U.S. Geological Survey. 2008. How streamflow is measured. *http://ga.water.usgs.gov/edu/measureflow.html*

Calculating Stream Discharge

Student Handout

Background

Streamflow, or discharge, is defined by the U.S. Geological Survey (USGS) as the volume of water flowing past a fixed point in a fixed unit of time. Stream discharge is measured in cubic feet per second or cubic meters per second. The discharge of a stream can be affected by many things, including topography and channel morphology. However, rainfall (the more rainfall there is, the greater the discharge) and land use have the greatest effect on stream discharge. Lack of vegetation increases surface runoff, whereas the presence of vegetation slows runoff. Being able to calculate stream discharge is important because this information is needed to make flood frequency predictions.

Objective

To measure the discharge of a stream.

Materials Needed Per Group

1. 3 pairs of waders
2. metric tape measure (at least 50 m)
3. meter stick
4. Vernier flow rate meter (see instructions below) with operating system

Method for Calculating Total Discharge of a Stream

First, find the area for each cell in the stream. This area can be calculated in the same way as the area of a trapezoid.

$$\text{Area} = \frac{(side + side)}{2}(width)$$

where the width is the width of each cell, which is 0.5 m or 1 m (this is the distance between depth readings), and the sides are the sides of each cell, which are the depth readings.

After finding the area for each cell, calculate the discharge for each cell:

$$\text{Discharge} = (area)\,(flow\ rate)$$

Find the total discharge for the stream by adding individual cell discharges together. If depth was measured in centimeters, convert it to meters when calculating the area.

Procedure

1. If not collecting stream data at this time, sit along the bank and record data. While waiting, begin working on calculations.
2. Select a section of the stream that does not have any debris, ripples, or meanders directly upstream from the site that will be measured.
3. Draw a cross section of the stream to record data on. See Figure 7.1 for an example of a cross section.

Figure 7.1. Cross Section of a Stream

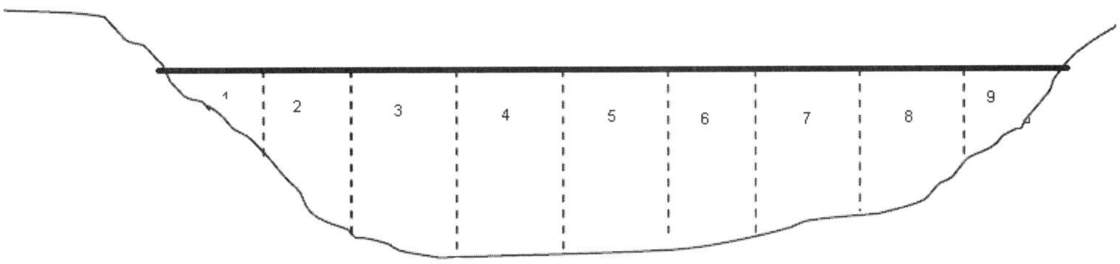

4. One student needs to stand in the stream at the bank holding one end of the tape measure while another student walks across the stream holding the other end of the tape measure. Hold the tape measure tightly above the stream surface and keep it in this position the entire time. This step is necessary to know where to take depth and flow rate measurements.
5. Once the tape measure is set up across the stream, a third student needs to measure the stream depth in meters every 0.5 m or 1.0 m, depending on the width of the stream (use 0.5 m for smaller streams). Read off the depth in centimeters and then convert to meters when recording the data if this is easier for you.
6. While stream depth is being measured, the other two students can begin measuring the flow rate. Place the propeller into the water in the middle of the water column; it should not be placed directly on the bottom or the top of the stream. Position the flow rate meter in between the 0.5 m depth readings so that the first flow rate will be collected at 0.25 m across the stream, the second at 0.75 m, and so on. Make sure that you and your classmates are standing downstream of the flow rate meter.
7. Record the data on the cross-sectional diagram of the stream. Write flow rates horizontally across the top of the cell and depths on the vertical dotted lines of the cell. Don't forget that the width of each cell is 0.5 m. If depths were recorded in centimeters, make sure to convert them to meters.
8. Answer the questions at the end of this handout.

Sample Calculation

The stream is divided into cells every 0.5 m. The depth of the cell is measured at both banks and at the boundaries of each cell. The flow rate is measured in the middle of each cell. A sample calculation for one cell is shown below:

$$\text{Area} = \frac{(0\text{ m} + 2\text{ m})}{2}(0.5\text{ m})$$

$$= 0.5\text{ m}^2$$

$$\text{Discharge} = (0.5\text{ m}^2)(0.001\text{ m/s})$$

$$= 0.0005\text{ m}^3\text{/s}$$

Name______________________________

Questions on Calculating Stream Discharge

1. Explain why it is important to monitor stream discharge.

____

____

____

2. Look at the following hydrographs, labeled A and B. Assuming that both streams have a similar-size watershed and rain event, explain what type of watershed (urbanized or nonurbanized) each hydrograph represents. Support your decision for both hydrographs.

____

____

____

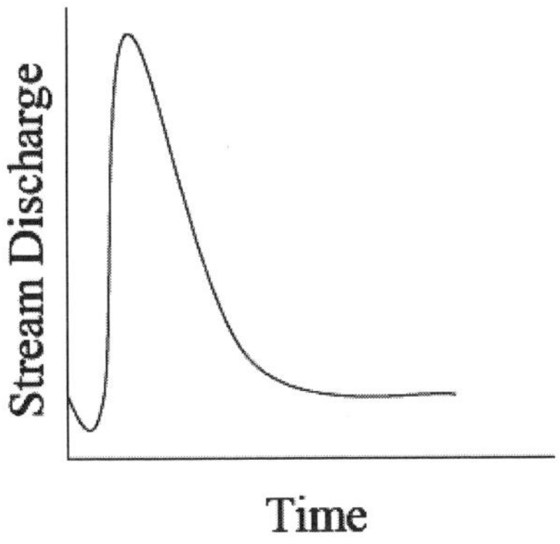

A

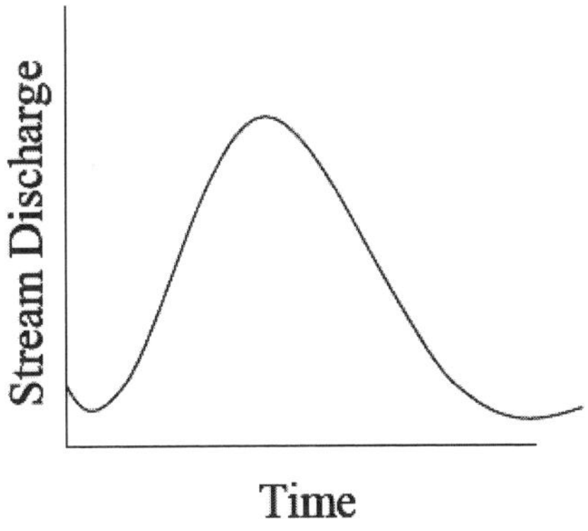

B

3. What was the total stream discharge? Remember to use correct units on the answer.

____

____

____

Attach the stream cross section complete with the data and the calculations that were performed to find total discharge.

CHAPTER 8

Flood Frequency Analysis for a River

Teacher Information

Background

In the 20th century, flooding was the most costly natural disaster in the United States (Perry 2000). In many watersheds, the frequency of flooding has greatly increased in the past 20 years, mainly due to changes in the hydrology as a result of farming and urbanization.

A *flood* is an event that occurs when a waterway overflows its banks. A *floodplain* is the flat area surrounding the banks of the waterway; this land area acts as a flood storage area (Fairfax County, 2008). Flooding is almost always a natural occurrence, with the exception of dam failure. Most floods occur on a seasonal basis and are caused by heavy rains.

Flash flooding produces a rapid rise in water within minutes to hours. Urban areas are most at risk for flash flooding because of impervious surfaces such as pavement, rooftops, and parking lots. Water runs off impervious surfaces very rapidly into waterways, causing the rapid rise in stream flow. For example, the Macatawa watershed in western Michigan typically does not see severe flash flooding because the area's overall topography is rather flat, but the watershed is considered to be "flashy" and frequently experiences high stream flows immediately after rainfall.

Historically, watersheds in the mid-latitude United States experienced spring flooding just as they do today. Many watersheds regularly see spring floods as snowmelt occurs and spring rains fall on saturated soil. As humans alter waterways with levees and clear and pave land, the volume of water in the waterways increases. With increased water volume, velocity and discharge increase simultaneously with erosion.

Flooding has many ecological benefits. Floods replenish wetlands, which serve as nurseries for fish, with water; wash wood debris into streams that fish use as habitat; and may limit invasive species because, unlike native species, invasives are not adapted to wet conditions brought on by floods (thus giving native plants an advantage). In addition, periodic flooding replenishes the surrounding floodplain land with nutrient-rich soil and transports sediments to coastal areas, maintaining coastal wetlands and deltas (Ecological Society of America 1998). Floodplain areas have always been desirable for farming because of the richness of the nutrients in the soil. However, human habitation of floodplains causes floods to be perceived as destructive. The actual destructiveness of a flood depends on what human interference there has been in the watershed and what humans have put in the floodplain area.

The U.S. Geological Survey (USGS) monitors the discharge of various streams throughout the United States. These data are now being collected electronically, which helps scientists forecast and manage floods and delineate floodplains (Wahl, Thomas, and Hirsch 1995). Most of us have heard the term "100-year flood." A 100-year flood does not only occur once every 100 years. In fact, in today's world 100-year floods are happening much more frequently. The term refers to the percent chance of a flood of that magnitude occurring each year. There is a 1% chance that a 100-year flood will occur in any given year. Two 100-year floods could occur in the same year, although this is highly unlikely.

As we continue to develop and change our watershed, large-scale flooding becomes more probable. A flood frequency analysis can predict the likelihood of a given flood in a given year, as well as the expected amount of discharge. This is valuable information for developers. For example, if a developer wanted to build by a river it would be important to know the chance of flooding. By constructing a flood frequency curve, the percent chance of any size flood can be predicted.

To calculate flood frequency, the annual exceedance probability (AEP) and recurrence interval (T) need to be calculated using a data set of peak flows for a given number of years. The annual exceedance probability is the probability that a given flow will be equaled or exceeded in any given year. It is written as a percentage and often referred to as percent chance. The recurrence interval is the number of years. For example, a 20-year flood has a recurrence interval of 20 years.

Objective

To predict the recurrence intervals and percent chance of various flows for a river.

Materials Needed Per Group

- data set for a river (see instructions below for obtaining this on the internet)
- access to computers

Obtaining a Data Set From the USGS Website for the Macatawa River

Go to the website *http://nwis.waterdata.usgs.gov/nwis* and select "Real-time Data." For the Macatawa River, click on Michigan in the map of the United States. Click on the dot on the boundary of Ottawa County and Allegan County (upon mouseover, it will show the site number 04108800, Macatawa River near Zeeland, MI). In the box that says "Available data for this site," find and select "Surface-water: Peak stream flow." Under output formats select "Table." The table that comes up will be the data set used in this investigation, but any data set for any watershed in the United States could be used. Copy the data into a spreadsheet for analysis.

Suggested Class Preparation and Format

This investigation is a good math-based earth science activity. It would be a good reinforcement activity when discussing flooding in any science class.

Obtaining the data set from the USGS website and learning how to perform the calculations will take a minimal amount of time. There is no lab setup involved.

This investigation will take one 50-minute class period. You may choose to omit the spreadsheet calculation and/or graphing tasks and supply the data to the students instead; if this is done, the activity will take less than a class period. Another option would be to have the students do a few of the calculations by hand before providing them with the data. Having the students enter the data and formulas into spreadsheet form and then make a graph does take extra time but gives the students practice in managing data.

Student Procedure

1. Paste the peak flow data (Q) and year, which were obtained from the USGS website, into a spreadsheet beginning with row 2 (leaving row 1 blank for headings). For now, place the years in column 1 and the peak flows in column 2; extra columns will be inserted later. Put the data in descending order by peak flow. (If using Excel, make sure the cursor is on the first cell of peak flow data, then click on Data on the toolbar. Select Sort and Descending. The years should rearrange as well.) Insert a column to the left of the years. In this column assign a rank number in a spreadsheet. (If using Excel, number the first cell 1, then click on the bottom right corner of the cell and drag down one cell. Stop dragging and hold the mouse still; a box should pop up. Click on this box and select Fill Series, then continue dragging the rank number down the column until each year and peak flow have been assigned a rank number.)
2. Insert a column in between the year and peak flow columns for recurrence interval. Calculate the recurrence interval (T) using the formula: $T = (n + 1) / m$, where m is the rank number and n is the total number of years in the data set. Put the formula into the spreadsheet. (If using Excel, click on the first cell in the recurrence interval column—this should be column 3 and row 2 [C2], provided row 1 was left for the heading. Click in the function box *fx* above the spreadsheet and enter the formula into the box. The formula should look like this when entered: "= (insert the total number of years of data here + 1) / A2". Once the formula is entered, press Enter and click and drag the formula down the column until the end of the data has been reached.)
3. Insert a column to the right of the peak flow column for the annual exceedance probability (AEP). Calculate the AEP by taking the inverse of the recurrence interval using the formula AEP = $m / (n + 1)$, Put the formula into the spreadsheet.
4. Make a semi-logarithmic graph of peak stream flow versus recurrence interval (instructions are below).

Making a Semi-Logarithmic Graph in Excel

With your peak flow data spreadsheet open, select Insert from the toolbar and click on Chart. Select XY Scatter Plot under Chart Type. Highlight the recurrence interval and peak flow columns for the data series to be graphed so that the recurrence interval is plotted on the x-axis and the peak flow is on the y-axis. Select Next, then enter the titles for the graph and axes. Select Next and Finish. Right-click on the x-axis, select Scale and check Logarithmic. Right-click on the graph and select Chart Options from the pop-up menu. Select the Gridlines tab and check the minor gridlines under the x-axis and major gridlines under the y-axis. To add a best-fit line, right-click on the graphed data and select Add Trendline, then select Logarithmic.

Sample Data

Table 8.1 contains the data set from the Macatawa River ranked according to peak stream flow, with AEP and *T* calculated. Give students this table if you choose to give them the data.

Table 8.1. Peak Flows for the Macatawa River

Rank	Year	Recurrence Interval (T)	Peak flow (Q) (cfs)	AEP
1	1997	46	8810	0.02173913
2	1981	23	7220	0.043478261
3	1982	15.33333333	4600	0.065217391
4	1996	11.5	4340	0.086956522
5	1979	9.2	4180	0.108695652
6	1989	7.666666667	4150	0.130434783
7	1978	6.571428571	3830	0.152173913
8	1994	5.75	3800	0.173913043
9	1973	5.111111111	3710	0.195652174
10	1985	4.6	3690	0.217391304
11	1980	4.181818182	3310	0.239130435
12	1983	3.833333333	3200	0.260869565
13	1984	3.538461538	3110	0.282608696
14	1991	3.285714286	3080	0.304347826
15	1986	3.066666667	3050	0.326086957
16	1966	2.875	2760	0.347826087
17	1976	2.705882353	2730	0.369565217
18	2000	2.555555556	2710	0.391304348
19	2001	2.421052632	2650	0.413043478
20	1974	2.3	2570	0.434782609
21	1965	2.19047619	2520	0.456521739
22	1993	2.090909091	2500	0.47826087
23	2002	2	2330	0.5
24	1999	1.916666667	2270	0.52173913
25	1995	1.84	2210	0.543478261
26	1971	1.769230769	2170	0.565217391
27	1972	1.703703704	2010	0.586956522
28	2005	1.642857143	1870	0.608695652
29	1963	1.586206897	1780	0.630434783
30	1962	1.533333333	1690	0.652173913
31	1967	1.483870968	1690	0.673913043
32	1975	1.4375	1660	0.695652174
33	1970	1.393939394	1570	0.717391304
34	2004	1.352941176	1530	0.739130435
35	1992	1.314285714	1520	0.760869565
36	1968	1.277777778	1370	0.782608696
37	1988	1.243243243	1320	0.804347826
38	1987	1.210526316	1240	0.826086957
39	1990	1.179487179	1220	0.847826087
40	1998	1.15	1180	0.869565217
41	1964	1.12195122	1130	0.891304348
42	2003	1.095238095	1040	0.913043478
43	1969	1.069767442	850	0.934782609
44	1977	1.045454545	728	0.956521739
45	1961	1.022222222	719	0.97826087

Note: AEP = annual exceedance probability; cfs = cubic feet per second.

Figure 8.1 is a semi-logarithmic XY scatter plot of peak flow versus time with a best-fit line added. If you choose not to have the students make the graph themselves, give them this figure to use in answering the questions on the handout.

Figure 8.1. Macatawa River Flood Frequency Curve

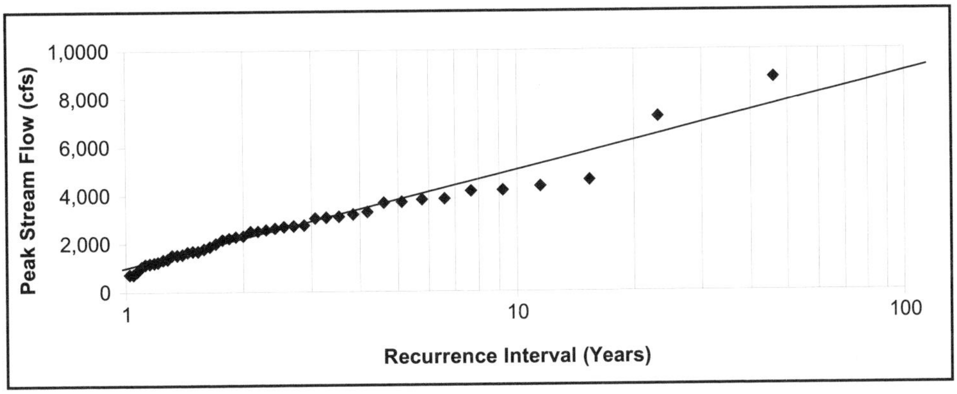

Answers to Questions in Student Handout (if using sample data from the Macatawa watershed)

1. 10-year: ~ 5,000 cfs; 25-year: ~ 6,500 cfs; 50-yr: ~ 7,700 cfs, 100-year: ~9,000 cfs (As USGS continues to add data, these numbers will change.)
2. usually 50 years
3. *T* = ~1.5 years; AEP = ~65% (Use the table to find these values.) erosion, increased phosphorus, increased eutrophication
4. 8,810 cfs in 1997
   AEP = 2%; *T* = 46 years (This is the answer students will get if they use the data table, because the table only has data for 45 years. This flood is probably a 200-year event.)
5. increased due to urbanization and drainage of wetlands
6. Put in flood storage areas like wetlands and retention/detention ponds.

References

Ecological Society of America. Fall 1998. *Flood and land management. www.esa.org/education/edupdfs/floods.pdf*

Fairfax County, Virginia. 2008. FAQs: *Floodplains. www.fairfaxcounty.gov/dpwes/navbar/faqs/floodplains.htm*

Perry, C. March 2000. *Significant floods in the United States during the 20th century—USGS measures a century of floods. USGS Fact Sheet 024-00. http://ks.water.usgs.gov/Kansas/pubs/fact-sheets/fs.024-00.html*

Wahl, K. L., W. O. Thomas Jr., and R. M. Hirsch. 1995. *An overview of the stream-gaging program.* USGS Fact Sheet FS-066-95. *http://water.usgs.gov/wid/html/SG.html*

Flood Frequency Analysis for a River

Student Handout

Background

In the 20th century, flooding was the most costly natural disaster in the United States. In many watersheds, the frequency of flooding has greatly increased in the past 20 years, mainly due to changes in the hydrology as a result of farming and urbanization.. Human habitation of floodplains causes floods to be perceived as destructive, but the actual destructiveness of a flood depends on what human interference there has been in the watershed and what humans have put in the floodplain area.

Objective

To predict the recurrence intervals and percent chance of various flows for a river.

Materials Needed Per Group

- data set for a river (available at *http://nwis.waterdata.usgs.gov/nwis*)
- access to computers

Procedure

1. Paste the peak flow data (*Q*) and year, which were obtained from the USGS website, into a spreadsheet beginning with row 2 (leaving row 1 blank for headings). For now, place the years in column 1 and the peak flows in column 2; extra columns will be inserted later. Put the data in descending order by peak flow. (If using Excel, make sure the cursor is on the first cell of peak flow data, then click on Data on the toolbar. Select Sort and Descending. The years should rearrange as well.) Insert a column to the left of the years. In this column assign a rank number in a spreadsheet. (If using Excel, number the first cell 1, then click on the bottom right corner of the cell and drag down one cell. Stop dragging and hold the mouse still; a box should pop up. Click on this box and select Fill Series, then continue dragging the rank number down the column until each year and peak flow have been assigned a rank number.)

Rank Number	Year	Recurrance Interval (T)	Peak flow (Q) (CFS)	Annual Exceedance Probability (AEP)
1	1997	46	8810	0.02173913

2. Insert a column in between the year and peak flow columns for recurrence interval. Calculate the recurrence interval (T) using the formula: $T = (n + 1) / m$, where m is the rank number and n is the total number of years in the data set. Put the formula into the spreadsheet. (If using Excel, click on the first cell in the recurrence interval column—this should be column 3 and row 2 [C2], provided row 1 was left for the heading. Click in the function box *fx* above the spreadsheet and enter the formula into the box. The formula should look like this when entered: " = (insert the total number of years of data here + 1) / A2". Once the formula is entered, press Enter and click and drag the formula down the column until the end of the data has been reached.)
3. Insert a column to the right of the peak flow column for the annual exceedance probability (AEP). Calculate the AEP by taking the inverse of the recurrence interval using the formula AEP = $m / (n + 1)$. Put the formula into the spreadsheet.
4. Make a semi-logarithmic graph of peak stream flow versus recurrence interval (instructions are below).
5. Answer the questions at the end of this handout.

SCILINKS
THE WORLD'S A CLICK AWAY

Topic: Flooding
Go to: *www.scilinks.org*
Code: WAT010

Topic: Rivers
Go to: *www.scilinks.org*
Code: WAT011

Making a Semi-Logarithmic Graph in Excel

With your peak flow data spreadsheet open, select Insert from the toolbar and click on Chart. Select XY Scatter Plot under Chart Type. Highlight the recurrence interval and peak flow columns for the data series to be graphed so that the recurrence interval is plotted on the x-axis and the peak flow is on the y-axis. Select Next, then enter the titles for the graph and axes. Select Next and Finish. Right-click on the x-axis, select Scale and check Logarithmic. Right-click on the graph and select Chart Options from the pop-up menu. Select the Gridlines tab and check the minor gridlines under the x-axis and major gridlines under the y-axis. To add a best-fit line, right-click on the graphed data and select Add Trendline, then select Logarithmic.

Name______________________________

Questions on Flood Frequency Analysis

Use the spreadsheet and graph to answer the following questions:

1. Using the flood frequency graph for the river, estimate the discharges (peak stream flow) of 10-year, 25-year, 50-year, and 100-year floods. Read the years off the x-axis and find the discharge that corresponds on the y-axis.

   10-year ____________________ 50-year ____________________

   25-year ____________________ 100-year ____________________

2. What is the recurrence interval of a 50-year flood?____________________

3. Approximately 1,500 cfs is needed to move sediment. Find the recurrence interval and the probability of this flow in any given year. What are the effects of increased sediment loads being transported down the river?

   ____

   ____

   ____

   ____

4. Since the USGS has been collecting data for the watershed, what was the highest peak stream flow and in what year did it occur? What are the probability and the recurrence interval of this discharge?

   ____

   ____

   ____

   ____

5. Look at the graph below, which shows peak stream flows from the Macatawa River. In general, have peak stream flows increased or decreased over the years? Give some reasons as to why or why not.

____

____

____

____

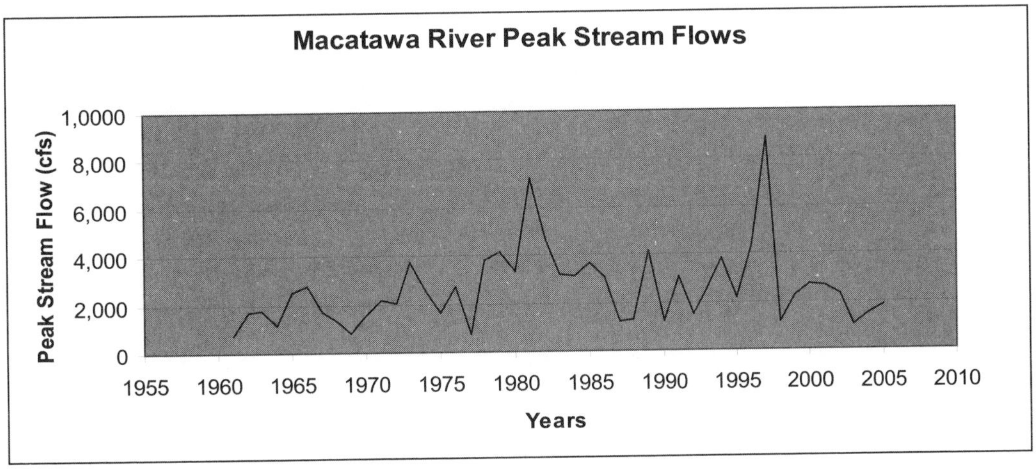

6. What can be done now to reduce flooding?

____

____

____

____

Comparison of Phosphate Levels in Stream Sediments

CHAPTER 9

Teacher Information

Background

Phosphorus is an important nutrient to all life. It is part of the backbone of the DNA molecule, and it is critical to the process by which energy is stored and used in the cell. For animals, phosphorus is an important component of bones and teeth. There are two basic forms of phosphorus as it cycles through nature (see Figure 9.1): inorganic phosphate, also called orthophosphate, and organic phosphate. Inorganic phosphate (PO_4^{3-}) is the only form plants can use. This phosphate ion is naturally released into the soil by the weathering of rocks, and from the soil it is taken up by plant roots. Plants and animals return phosphate to the soil as organic phosphate. Organic phosphate is not usable by plants, but it is slowly changed back into inorganic phosphate through mineralization by bacteria (U.S. Environmental Protection Agency [EPA] 2006).

Figure 9.1. The Phosphorus Cycle

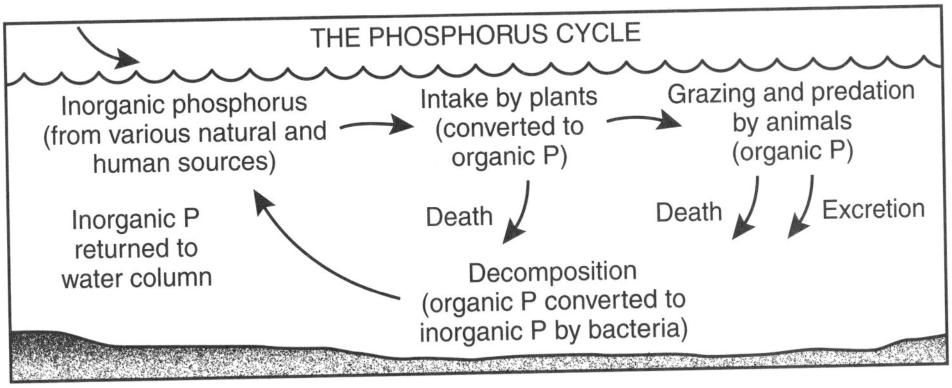

Because phosphorus is vital to living organisms, it is considered a plant macronutrient. Farmers use fertilizers that contain inorganic phosphates on their fields to increase their crop yield, and homeowners apply phosphates for plush green lawns. Unfortunately, when phosphate is added to fields or lawns it is not entirely used up by the plants; some phosphate will remain on the soil. Phosphate anions that are "leftover" readily bind to clay particles because of cations like Al^{3+} and Ca^{2+} that are in the soil. These bound inorganic phosphates can transport easily with loose soil.

As a result, phosphate enters waterways mainly through surface runoff. The phosphate can be bound to the sediments in the runoff or dissolved directly in the water. There is very little problem with phosphate leaching through the soil into the groundwater because of the binding capacity of the soil and the low solubility of phosphate in water. Although phosphate that is bound to sediment is unusable by plants, the phosphate may reenter the water column under anoxic conditions. Figure 9.2 illustrates the different ways phosphorus can enter water.

Figure 9.2. Potential Pathways for Phosphate Loss From Agricultural Fields or Residential Lawns

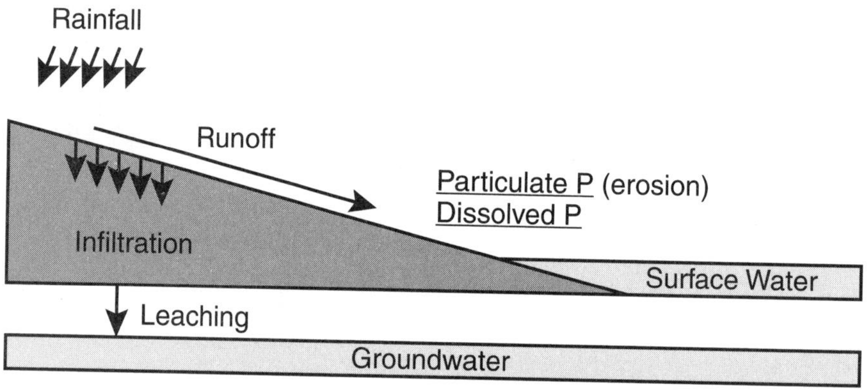

From the colonial period to the early 1900s, the majority of the land in the United States was used for farming. Beginning in the late 1800s, farmers applied phosphate to increase crop yield—in some cases as much as 500 lb of superphosphate fertilizer per acre of land (*Holland City News* 1879). It can be assumed that even though land use has changed, soils have the potential to be high in phosphate because of previous farming practices. This phosphate enters the watershed when flash flooding caused by urbanization leads to high rates of erosion.

In a process known as *eutrophication*, algae growth is seriously affected by the excess phosphate entering the watershed. Phosphorus is the "limiting reagent" for growth for most algae, so nuisance algal blooms often occur when there is excess bioavailable phosphate entering a watershed. The overproduction of algae blocks out sunlight for the deeper water plants, often killing them. When the algae die off after a bloom, the excessive decay on the bottom of a waterway often uses up all the available oxygen, and this lack of oxygen can kill the fish in the waterway as well. Basically, eutrophication is a stress on the entire ecosystem because of an excess nutrient introduced into the watershed. Measuring phosphate levels accurately in water and sediments is the first step in understanding the ecological health of eutrophic watersheds.

Objective

To analyze phosphate levels in stream sediments by land use area.

Materials Needed Per Group

- access to streams in farming and nonfarming locations
- 500 ml sampling bottles (as many as needed for sample size)
- trowel
- spectrophotometer (if not available, see "Optional Extensions" section)
- ~ 1 L of 1 M HCl (hydrochloric acid) for acid washing labware
- KH_2PO_4 (potassium phosphate, dibasic) for making phosphate standards
- 70 ml of 18 M H_2SO_4 (sulfuric acid)
- 1.3715 g of $C_8H_4K_2O_{12}Sb_2.3H_2O$ (antimony potassium tartrate)
- 20 g of $(NH_4)_2MoO_4$ (ammonium molybdate)
- 5.28 g of $C_6H_8O_6$ (ascorbic acid)
- 1 drop of phenolphthalein indicator
- ~ 3 L of deionized (DI) water (or any type of purified water)
- goggles (for laboratory procedures only)
- waders (optional)
- graphing calculator (optional)

Suggested Class Preparation and Format

This investigation would work well in a biology or advanced biology class when studying water quality issues. It could also be used in an earth science class when studying the different minerals in the soil.

The combined reagent solution must be prepared ahead of time. The solution lasts approximately one week. In addition, all glassware will have to be acid-washed (washed with 1 M HCl) to test for phosphate. This will take about 10 minutes and can be done by the students the day before the investigation. Equipment setup is minimal.

You may give students a traditional set of instructions (Student Handout A) or use a more open-ended exploratory investigation, in which only the methods are explained and students must design their own set of experiments and methods (Student Handout B). If the traditional approach is used, the investigation could be run in four 50-minute class periods: one for collecting soil samples, one for setting up the tests, one for running the phosphate tests, and one for analyzing results. If the inquiry approach is used, you will need an additional class period for students to conduct background research and design the experiment.

SCILINKS. THE WORLD'S A CLICK AWAY
Topic: pH
Go to: *www.scilinks.org*
Code: WAT012

Stream soil samples should be collected from a variety of farming and nonfarming areas. Students could collect these samples during class time, or they could be assigned to collect their own samples from a stream outside of class. Caution them not to go into deep water.

The stream sediment samples will contain organic phosphate and inorganic phosphate. The method for testing phosphate included here measures inorganic phosphate (orthophosphate). Both organic and inorganic phosphate can be dissolved in the water or attached to sediments (EPA 2006). The procedure in this analysis assumes that inorganic phosphate attached to the collected stream sediments will dissolve into the DI water added in the laboratory. Not all of the phosphate attached to the stream sediments will dissolve into the water; therefore, this procedure should only be used as a method to make comparisons of phosphate levels between samples.

This phosphate analysis can also be used for determining phosphate concentration of water samples if performing water quality tests. Most of the phosphate kits available on the market for water quality testing are not sensitive enough to measure phosphate because they measure in parts per million instead of parts per billion.

Methods

Acid-Washing Labware

To properly run a phosphate analysis, it is important that all labware used in the investigation be acid-washed to remove all traces of phosphate left by detergents. You can do this ahead of time, or students can wash labware on an as-needed basis.

Pour 3–5 ml of 1 M HCl into the glassware to be washed. Swirl the acid around the glassware, and rotate the glassware so the acid covers the entire interior surface. To conserve acid, pour it into a receptacle set aside for the acid so it can be reused. Rinse the labware with acid two more times in this fashion, then rinse the labware three times with DI water in the same fashion. The DI wastewater can go down the drain.

Collecting a Stream Soil Sample

Have students obtain 30 g of stream sediment and place it into an acid-washed 500 ml sampling bottle labeled with the site location. Students should enter the stream carefully, making sure not to enter into deep water. If the water is too deep, the soil sample should be obtained near the edge. If the water is shallow, the soil sample should be obtained near the middle. Have the students use the trowel to fill the bottle half-full with sediments from the bottom of the stream and then cap the bottle. After returning to the classroom, have students add enough DI water to fill up the bottle (approximately 300 ml), shake the contents, and allow the sediment to settle out overnight. The students will be using the water from the sediment sample to run the phosphate analysis. If the samples will not be used within 24 hours, they should be refrigerated.

Testing for Inorganic Phosphate

Making the Combined Reagent Solution

1. Add 70 ml of 18 M sulfuric acid very slowly to 430 ml of DI water. This solution will have a concentration of 2.5 M.
   CAUTION: Concentrated sulfuric acid is a very corrosive and dangerous chemical, and this dilution is exothermic so the beaker will become very hot. Take all necessary precautions when handling sulfuric acid. Add the acid to the water; NEVER add water to acid. If any of the acid is spilled while making the solution, neutralize immediately with a base. When disposing of excess acid, neutralize it first with base. DO NOT POUR ACID DOWN THE SINK.
2. Weigh out 1.4 g of antimony potassium tartrate and dissolve in 500 ml of DI water.
3. Weigh out 20 g of ammonium molybdate and dissolve in 500 ml of DI water.
4. Weigh out 5.28 g of ascorbic acid and dissolve in 300 ml of DI water. This solution should be clear or a pale yellow color.
5. Mix together in an Erlenmeyer flask 500 ml of the 2.5 M sulfuric acid solution, 50 ml of the antimony potassium tartrate solution, 150 ml of the ammonium molybdate solution, and 300 ml of the ascorbic acid solution. This will produce 1,000 ml of combined reagent solution. The combined reagent solution, which is a pale yellow, will last for one week and should be refrigerated when not in use. A pale yellow solution that begins to turn blue indicates contamination of phosphate by glassware that was not acid-washed properly; if this occurs, the combined reagent will have to be remade.

Running the Phosphate Analysis

1. Prepare five standard solutions of increasing known concentration of phosphate content. For directions on how to make the standards, refer to the EPA website listed in the "References" section or, for more specific directions, *ocw.kfupm.edu.sa/user062/CE37051/Phosphate%20procedure.doc*
2. Measure out 25 ml of known phosphate concentration sample into a 125 ml flask.
3. Add one drop of phenolphthalein indicator to your sample and swirl to mix. If a pink color develops, add hydrolyzing acid (2.5 M sulfuric acid will work fine) dropwise until the color disappears.
4. Add 4.0 ml of the combined reagent solution. Swirl to mix.
5. Set the solution aside and begin the stopwatch. Let the color develop for 10–30 minutes (you choose the time frame).
6. As the color develops, repeat steps 2–5 for the rest of the known phosphate concentration samples. While the color is developing, calibrate the spectrophotometer that will be used to determine the absorbance using DI water as your blank sample. Use 700–880 nm for the wavelength.

7. Rinse a cuvette twice with DI water and then twice with the digested known solution (*digested* refers to the standard solution having been mixed with the combined reagent and the blue color having been developed). After the rinse, fill the cuvette two-thirds of the way with the digested known phosphate concentration solution and place it in the spectrophotometer to determine its absorbance. Repeat these steps until the absorbance of all known solutions have been determined.
8. Repeat steps 2–7 for the unknown samples. Make sure to use an undigested sample of the unknown to calibrate the spectrophotometer.
9. Determine the phosphate concentration for the unknown samples using a Beer's law plot (see instructions in next section).

Obtaining a Beer's Law Plot

1. On a Texas Instruments (TI) graphing calculator, press the STAT button and then select Edit.
2. A spreadsheet will appear on the screen. Enter the concentrations of the known phosphate standards into L1. These are the x-values. Enter the absorbance values of each standard into L2. These are the y-values.
3. Press STAT again and move over to the CALC tab. From this menu, select "LinReg(ax+b)" and press Enter. This will run a linear regression of the standard data. The a-value is the slope of the line, and the b-value is the y-intercept of the line. Record these values on a sheet of paper.
4. The unknown absorbance data obtained from the spectrophotometer corresponds to the y variable in the Beer's law plot. To determine the phosphate concentrations of the unknown samples, first solve this formula for the x variable. On the graphing calculator press the "Y=" button to enter the graph menu. In the "Y1=" line, type in "(X - B) /A." For the B and A variables enter the values calculated in step 3.
5. Press 2nd and then Trace. From this new menu, select Value. A graph of the line will be displayed, and "X=" will be at the bottom corner of the screen. Type in the first unknown absorbance value and press Enter. A cursor will be taken to that point on the line. In the lower right corner of the screen, a "Y=" value will be displayed. This value is the phosphate concentration that corresponds to the typed-in absorbance. Record this concentration value in a table or Excel spreadsheet.
6. Repeat step 5 for each unknown to determine the phosphate concentration for each sample.

For a more traditional approach without graphing calculators or computer spreadsheets, the Beer's law plot can be obtained by hand on graph paper by plotting the concentration of the standards (in parts per billion) on the x-axis and the measured absorbance values on the y-axis. A best-fit line (by eye) will often give very reasonable results, where unknown concentrations read off the y-axis can have the corresponding concentration interpolated off the x-axis.

Sample Data

As shown in Table 9.1 and Figure 9.3, total orthophosphate levels in the stream sediments in both farming and nonfarming areas are very high. Normal phosphate levels should be less than 30 ppb. The average phosphate level for farming areas is 605 ppb, and the average for nonfarming areas is 247 ppb. Although the phosphate level in farming areas is usually higher (as can be expected from surface runoff), the phosphate level in nonfarming areas (while usually lower when compared with farming areas) is much higher than normal levels should be. The high levels of phosphate found in nonfarming area stream sediments may be due to erosion of sediments in areas that were historically farmed and are still high in phosphates; or, in some cases, the high phosphate levels may be from sediments carried from upstream farming areas.

Table 9.1. Total Orthophosphate Levels in Stream Sediments in Farming and Nonfarming Areas

Site Name	Absorbance	Concentration (ppb)	Description of Land Use	Description of Soil
Site #1 @ 144th	0.503	961	Farming	Clay, silty, lots of vegetation in water
S. Branch @ 55th	0.230	249	Farming	Clay, silty, sandy with rocks
88th & Adams	0.326	499	Nonfarming, residential	Mucky, vegetation
New Groningen Cem.	0.188	139	Nonfarming, residential	Mucky
Paw Paw Park	0.264	337	Nonfarming, park	Mucky
Van Raalte Park	0.178	113	Nonfarming, park	Sandy, rocky bottom
72nd by Cemetery	0.236	264	Nonfarming in immediate vicinity, wooded	Streambed dry
Cedar Creek	0.316	473	Nonfarming, residential	Mucky
Pine Creek @ Ott Beach	0.165	78.8	Nonfarming, park	Sandy with dark sediment layer on top in areas
Harlem Drain	0.174	102	Nonfarming, park and residential	Sandy, lots of vegetation
Brower Drain	0.215	209	Nonfarming, residential and industrial	Sandy with muck layer, vegetation
Mac River behind Sunrise Dr.	0.231	251	Nonfarming, residential	Mucky

Figure 9.3 Total Inorganic Orthophosphate Levels in Stream Sediments in Farming and Nonfarming Areas

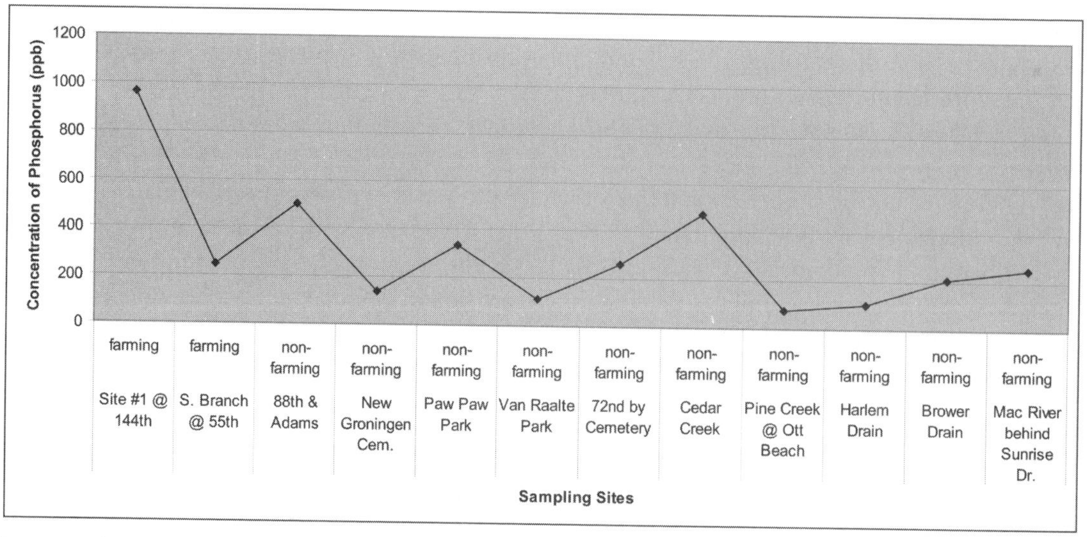

Optional Extensions

- Students can prepare a Beer's law plot with a computer or by hand on graph paper instead of on a graphing calculator.
- If a spectrophotometer is not available, prepare the known concentration of phosphate standards ahead of time. Then prepare a similar-color blue standard using blue dye and water. Student can compare their unknown colors to the blue dye standards. (The known concentration of phosphate standards cannot be used because the color continues to develop and then degrade.)
- In place of the chemical test for phosphate, a commercial soil test kit can be used to test for phosphate content. For example, Hach (*www.hach.com*) sells field test kits with which soils are compared to a color wheel to obtain approximate phosphate concentrations.

Answers to Questions in Student Handouts

1. Answers will vary.
2. Answers will vary. Phosphate in farming areas comes from surface runoff. Levels depend on when a farmer has applied the fertilizer. In nonfarming areas the phosphate may be due to historical land use of farming or may be coming in from upstream farming areas.
3. Excess phosphate lowers the quality of water through the excess of aquatic plant growth in lakes. The plants are decomposed by bacteria that use up oxygen in the water, thereby lowering the oxygen levels in the lake. Lower oxygen levels adversely affect animal life in the lake.

References

U.S. Environmental Protection Agency (EPA). November 2006. 5.6 Phosphorus. *www.epa.gov/volunteer/stream/vms56.html*

Holland City News. 1879. September 6. [Article accessed at Joint Archives of Holland, Holland, MI; no author or title.]

Comparison of Phosphate Levels in Stream Sediments

Student Handout A

Background

Phosphorus is an important nutrient to all life. There are two basic forms of phosphorus as it cycles through nature: inorganic phosphate, also called orthophosphate; and organic phosphate. Inorganic phosphate (PO_4^{3-}) is the only form plants can use. Because phosphorus is vital to living organisms, it is considered a plant macronutrient. Farmers use fertilizers or manures that contain phosphates on their fields to increase their crop yield, and homeowners apply phosphate fertilizer for green lawns. Unfortunately, when phosphate reaches the soil it is not all used up by the plants. If excess phosphate enters the waterways in the watershed, it can cause increased plant growth in lakes and streams and lead to the eutrophication of lakes.

Objective

To analyze phosphate levels in stream sediments by land use area.

Materials

- access to streams in farming and nonfarming locations
- sampling bottles (500 ml)
- trowel
- spectrophotometer
- phenolphthalein indicator
- ~ 3 L of deionized (DI) water (or any type of purified water)
- goggles (for laboratory procedures only)
- waders (optional)

Methods

Acid-Washing Labware

To properly run a phosphate analysis, it is important that all labware used in the investigation be acid-washed to remove all traces of phosphate left by detergents. Your teacher can do this ahead of time, or you can wash labware on an as-needed basis.

Pour 3–5 ml of 1 M hydrochloric acid (HCl) into the glassware to be washed. Swirl the acid around the glassware, and rotate the glassware so the acid covers the entire interior surface. To conserve acid, pour it into a receptacle set aside for the acid so it can be reused. Rinse the labware with the acid two more times in this fashion, and then rinse the labware three times with DI water in the same fashion. The DI wastewater can go down the drain.

Collecting a Stream Soil Sample

1. Label an acid-washed 500 ml sampling bottle with the site location. Record stream location, land use, and description of soil on the table in your answer sheet.
2. Enter the stream carefully, making sure not to enter into deep water. If the water is too deep, obtain the soil sample near the edge. If the water is shallow, obtain the soil sample near the middle. Using a trowel, fill the bottle half-full with sediments from the bottom of the stream. Cap the bottle.
3. Add 300 ml of DI water to the sediment and shake. Cap the bottle and allow the sediments to settle out overnight. Bottles can be kept at room temperature if used within 24 hours; otherwise, they should be refrigerated until you are ready to perform the analysis.

Running the Phosphate Analysis

1. Prepare five standard solutions of increasing known concentration of phosphate content.
2. Measure out 25 ml of known phosphate concentration sample into a 125 ml flask.
3. Add one drop of phenolphthalein indicator to your sample and swirl to mix. If a pink color develops, add hydrolyzing acid dropwise until the color disappears.
4. Add 4.0 ml of the combined reagent solution. Swirl to mix.
5. Set the solution aside and begin the stopwatch. Let the color develop for 10–30 minutes (your teacher will decide what time frame to use).
6. As the color develops, repeat steps 2–5 for the rest of the known phosphate concentration samples. While the color is developing, calibrate the spectrophotometer that will be used to determine the absorbance using DI water as your blank sample. Use 700–880 nm for the measurement wavelength.
7. Rinse a cuvette twice with DI water and then twice with the digested known solution (*digested* refers to the standard solution having been mixed with the combined reagent and the blue color having been developed). After the rinse, fill the cuvette two-thirds of the way with the digested known phosphate concentration solution and place it in the spectrophotometer to determine its absorbance. Record the data on the table in your answer sheet. Repeat these steps until the absorbance of all known standards have been determined.
8. Repeat steps 1–7 for the unknown samples.
9. Determine the phosphate concentration for the unknown samples using a Beer's Law plot (see instructions in next section).

Obtaining a Beer's Law Plot Using a TI Graphing Calculator

1. On your TI graphing calculator, press the STAT button and then select Edit.
2. You will see what looks like a spreadsheet. Enter the concentrations of the known phosphate standards into L1. These are your x-values. Enter the absorbance values of each standard into L2. These are your y-values.
3. Press STAT again and move over to the CALC tab. From this menu, select "LinReg(ax+b)" and press Enter. This will run a linear regression of your standard data. The a-value is the slope of your line, and the b-value is the y-intercept of your line. Record these values on a sheet of paper.
4. The unknown absorbance data obtained from the spectrophotometer corresponds to the *y* variable in the Beer's law plot. To determine the phosphate concentrations of the unknown samples, first solve this formula for the x variable. On the graphing calculator press the "Y=" button to enter the graph menu. In the "Y1=" line, type in "(X – B) / A". For the *B* and *A* variables enter the values calculated in step 3.
5. Press 2nd and then Trace. From this new menu, select Value. A graph of the line will be displayed, and "X=" will be at the bottom corner of the screen. Type in the first unknown absorbance value and press Enter. A cursor will be taken to that point on the line. In the lower right corner of the screen, a "Y=" value will be displayed. This value is the phosphate concentration that corresponds to the typed-in absorbance. Record this concentration value in a table or Excel spreadsheet.
6. Repeat step 5 for each unknown to determine the phosphate concentration for each sample.

Name______________________________

Comparison of Phosphate Levels in Stream Sediments

Phosphate Levels in Stream Sediments in Farming and Nonfarming Areas

Site Name and Location	Absorbance	Concentration (ppb)	Description of Land Use	Description of Soil

1. Find the average concentration of phosphate for farming areas and nonfarming areas.

____

____

____

____

2. Are farming and nonfarming areas contributing a significant amount of phosphate to the watershed? Explain where this phosphate may be coming from.

____

____

____

____

3. Explain how excess phosphate lowers water quality.

____

____

____

____

Attach Beer's Law plot and a graph of concentration versus land use to this handout.

Comparison of Phosphate Levels in Stream Sediments

Student Handout B

Objective

To analyze phosphate levels in stream sediments by land use area.

In this investigation, phosphate levels in stream sediments will be analyzed by land use area. Phosphate makes its way into our waterways through surface runoff and leads to the eutrophication of lakes. Phosphate can enter surface runoff from land used for agricultural purposes or as a result of use of fertilizers by homeowners, failed septic systems, and erosion of sediment.

The first step in designing this lab investigation is to define a hypothesis. An example of a hypothesis is as follows: *Phosphate levels in stream soil sediments will be higher in farming area than in nonfarming areas.*

State your hypothesis.

____

____

____

____

How will you test this hypothesis using the equipment and methods listed in this handout? Think about the following questions:

1. What types of data should be collected to test the hypothesis?
2. What will you use as a control?
3. How many trials should there be?
4. How will you find streams in farming areas and in nonfarming areas?
5. How will evaporation be reduced in your samples?

Write down a step-by-step procedure, and create a spreadsheet for the results. Set up the experiment after the teacher has approved your procedure. When data collection is complete, enter it into a spreadsheet and into graph form. Then answer the questions at the end of this handout.

Materials

- access to streams in farming and nonfarming locations
- sampling bottles (500 ml)
- trowel
- spectrophotometer
- phenolphthalein indicator
- ~ 3 L of deionized (DI) water (or any type of purified water)
- goggles (for laboratory procedures only)
- waders (optional)

Methods

Acid-Washing Labware

To properly run a phosphate analysis, it is important that all labware used in the investigation be acid-washed to remove all traces of phosphate left by detergents. Your teacher can do this ahead or time, or you can wash labware on an as-needed basis.

Pour 3–5 ml of 1 M hydrochloric acid (HCl) into the glassware to be washed. Swirl the acid around the glassware, and rotate the glassware so the acid covers the entire interior surface. To conserve acid, pour it into a receptacle set aside for the acid so it can be reused. Rinse the labware with the acid two more times in this fashion, and then rinse the labware three times with DI water in the same fashion. The DI wastewater can go down the drain.

Collecting a Stream Soil Sample

1. Label an acid-washed 500 ml sampling bottle with the site location. Record stream location, land use, and description of soil on your spreadsheet.
2. Enter the stream carefully, making sure not to enter into deep water. If the water is too deep, obtain the soil sample near the edge. If the water is shallow, obtain the soil sample near the middle. Using a trowel, fill the bottle half-full with sediments from the bottom of the stream. Cap the bottle.
3. Add 300 mL of DI water to the sediment and shake. Cap the bottle and allow the sediments to settle overnight. Bottles can be kept at room temperature if used within 24 hours; otherwise, they should be refrigerated until you are ready to perform the analysis.

Testing for Inorganic Phosphate: Running the Phosphate Analysis

1. Prepare five standard solutions of increasing known concentration of phosphate content.
2. Measure out 25 ml of known phosphate concentration sample into a 125 ml flask.
3. Add one drop of phenolphthalein indicator to your sample and swirl to mix. If a pink color develops, add hydrolyzing acid dropwise until the color disappears.

4. Add 4.0 ml of the combined reagent solution. Swirl to mix.
5. Set the solution aside and begin the stopwatch. Let the color develop for 10–30 minutes.
6. As the color develops, repeat steps 2–5 for the rest of the known phosphate concentration samples. While the color is developing, calibrate the spectrophotometer that will be used to determine the absorbance with DI water. Use 700–880 nm for the measurement wavelength.
7. Rinse a cuvette twice with DI water and then twice with the digested known solution (*digested* refers to the standard solution having been mixed with the combined reagent and the blue color having been developed). After the rinse, fill the cuvette two-thirds of the way with the digested known phosphate concentration solution and place it in the spectrophotometer to determine its absorbance. Repeat these steps until the absorbance of all known standards have been determined.
8. Repeat steps 2–7 for the unknown samples.
9. Determine the phosphate concentration for the unknown samples using a Beer's law plot.

Obtaining a Beer's Law Plot Using a TI Graphing Calculator

1. On your TI graphing calculator, press the STAT button and then select Edit.
2. You will see what looks like a spreadsheet. Enter the concentrations of the known phosphate standards into L1. These are your x-values. Enter the absorbance values of each standard into L2. These are your y-values.
3. Press STAT again and move over to the CALC tab. From this menu, select "LinReg(ax+b)" and press Enter. This will run a linear regression of your standard data. The a-value is the slope of your line, and the b-value is the y-intercept of your line. Record these values on a sheet of paper.
4. The unknown absorbance data obtained from the spectrophotometer corresponds to the *y* variable in the Beer's law plot. To determine the phosphate concentrations of the unknown samples, first solve this formula for the x variable. On the graphing calculator press the "Y=" button to enter the graph menu. In the "Y1=" line, type in "(X – B) / A". For the *B* and *A* variables enter the values calculated in step 3.
5. Press 2nd and then Trace. From this new menu, select Value. A graph of the line will be displayed, and "X=" will be at the bottom corner of the screen. Type in the first unknown absorbance value and press Enter. A cursor will be taken to that point on the line. In the lower right corner of the screen, a "Y=" value will be displayed. This value is the phosphate concentration that corresponds to the typed-in absorbance. Record this concentration value in a table or Excel spreadsheet.
6. Repeat step 5 for each unknown to determine the phosphate concentration for each sample.

Name____________________________

Questions on Phosphate Levels in Stream Sediments

1. Find the average concentration of phosphate for farming areas and nonfarming areas.

____

____

____

____

2. Are farming and nonfarming areas contributing a significant amount of phosphate to the watershed? Explain where this phosphate may be coming from.

____

____

____

____

3. Explain how excess phosphate lowers water quality.

____

____

____

____

CHAPTER 10

Aquatic Macroinvertebrate Identification

Teacher Information

Background

Everyone is familiar with terrestrial insects such as dragonflies, houseflies, mosquitoes, and beetles, but many of us are unaware that many insects live in the water during their larval stages. These insects are part of a larger group of organisms called *aquatic macroinvertebrates,* which also includes crustaceans, worms, and mollusks. They are called macroinvertebrates because they can be seen with the naked eye and lack vertebrae. The information that follows focuses only on aquatic insects.

SCILINKS. THE WORLD'S A CLICK AWAY
Topic: Invertebrate Animals
Go to: *www.scilinks.org*
Code: WAT013

Aquatic insects can undergo a complete or an incomplete metamorphosis. In *complete metamorphosis* (Figure 10.1), the egg hatches and the larva emerges. During the larval stage the insect grows into a pupa, which in turn grows into the adult. The larva and pupa do not look like the adult. Aquatic insects that go through complete metamorphosis include beetles, caddisflies, dobsonflies, and true flies.

Figure 10.1. Complete Metamorphosis

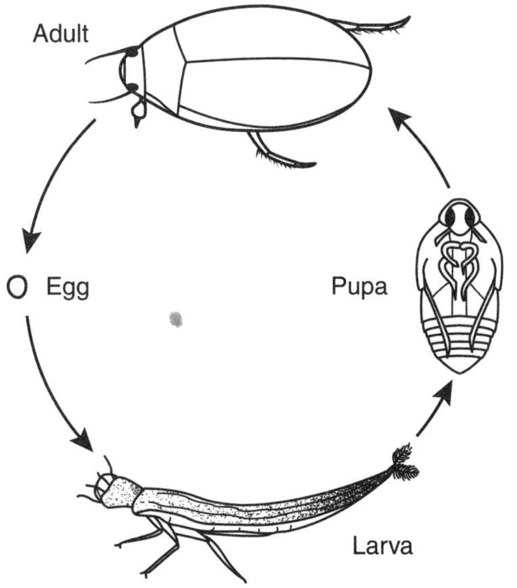

Used with permission from *www.umd.umich.edu/eic/aquatic_insecta/insect_metamorphosis.htm*

Aquatic insect eggs that go through *incomplete metamorphosis* hatch into nymphs and then the nymphs mature into the adult insects (Figure 10.2). The nymphs look similar to the adults. Nymphs have exoskeletons that they molt several times before emerging as adults. Aquatic insects that go through incomplete metamorphosis include mayflies, dragonflies, damselflies, stoneflies, and true bugs.

Figure 10.2. Incomplete Metamorphosis

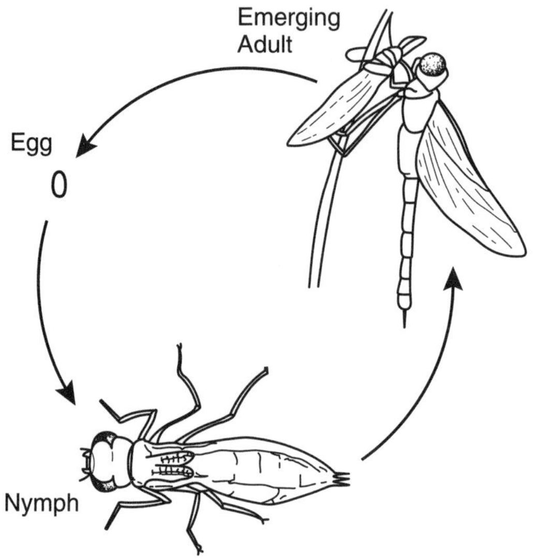

Used with permission from *www.umd.umich.edu/eic/aquatic_insecta/insect_metamorphosis.htm*

SCiLINKS
THE WORLD'S A CLICK AWAY
Topic: Aquatic Ecosystems
Go to: *www.scilinks.org*
Code: WAT014

Terrestrial insects have three body parts: the head, the thorax, and the abdomen. Adult insects have an exoskeleton, a protective covering that is periodically shed as they grow (University of Michigan Dearborn n.d.). Aquatic insects can be grouped according to the type of movement of the immature insects, feeding behavior of the immature insects, habitat, pollution sensitivity, metamorphosis, and feeding preferences (see *www.lamotte.com/pages/edu/pdf/insects.pdf.* for a chart with this information).

Aquatic insects almost always inhabit freshwater and not marine ecosystems. There are eight orders of aquatic insects: Ephemeroptera (mayflies), Odonata (dragonflies and damselflies), Plecoptera (stoneflies), Hemiptera (true bugs), Megaloptera (alderflies, fishflies, and dobsonflies), Coleoptera (beetles and weevils), Trichoptera (caddisflies) and Diptera (true flies, which include mosquitoes, midges, and black flies) (Singletary, McGinley, and Bledzki 2008). These organisms are easy to collect and identify. A nice catalog of pictures of many different kinds of aquatic macroinvertebrates can be found at *www.bgsd.k12.wa.us/hml/jr_cam/macros/amc/index.html.*

Aquatic insects have many adaptations that enable them to survive in their freshwater habitats; only a few of these adaptations are highlighted here. Mayflies, dragonflies, damselflies, stoneflies, and dobsonflies all have gills so they can obtain oxygen.

The gills on mayflies and stoneflies are easy to see. Some species of mayflies have gills that run along their abdomens on the outside of their bodies, and these gills can be seen "beating" in the water. Dragonflies have their gills inside their abdomen, and water is continually pumped through the abdomen out its posterior end. The dragonfly can use this as method of jet propulsion to make a quick getaway if needed. Most of the true bugs spend their entire life cycle in the aquatic environment and obtain oxygen by surfacing and carrying bubbles of oxygen under their wings or on hairs. All true bugs have piercing, sucking mouth parts, which the bug uses to liquefy the inside of its prey (Singletary, McGinley, and Bledzki 2008).

Aquatic macroinvertebrates make up the basis of the food web of streams and wetlands and are great indicators of water quality. Each species has a different level of pollution tolerance, with some species being very sensitive to and others extremely tolerant of pollution. The website *www.roaringfork.org/images/other/aquaticinvertebratesheet.pdf* groups the aquatic macroinvertebrates according to pollution tolerance.

Objective

To identify common macroinvertebrates that live in streams and wetlands.

Materials Needed Per Pair of Students

- access to stream and/or pond
- dip net (D-frame dip nets work best) for streams or wetlands or kick net for streams
- tweezers
- shallow pan
- dichotomous key for macroinvertebrates in streams and ponds
- dissecting scope
- informational note cards about insects (make your own or order a set from a science catalog)

Suggested Class Preparation and Format

Students of all ages love collecting insects. This investigation could be done with any class for exposure to outdoor learning. Most likely it would be used in a biology class when discussing insects. It could also be used in an environmental science class studying water quality, because macroinvertebrates are great indicators of the health of a stream.

Very little setup is required for this investigation if you are experienced with collecting and identifying aquatic macroinvertebrates. If you have not had prior training, be sure to visit the site ahead of time to collect and identify some of the organisms first.

One class period indoors should be used to teach the students about the organisms they will be collecting by setting up samples of the aquatic invertebrates with dissecting scopes and note cards containing identifying characteristics about each. If you are just starting out and do not have a collection of organisms, pictures of the aquatic macroinvertebrates could be used instead.

At least one more class period will be needed for collecting the insects. Students could collect them in one day or over several days. Students could collect and identify the organisms in the field or preserve them in alcohol and return to the classroom to identify them at a later date. If you plan on conducting sampling routinely, we suggest that the organisms be sampled and then released. To help motivate students when they are collecting, you can give the class goals (e.g., they need to collect 10 different species) and then give student points based on the number collected. Once students can identify the macroinvertebrates, you can give them a list of species they need to find. Students could keep the organisms in a jar until the end of the hour and then bring them up to you to confirm identification. If both a stream and a pond habitat are available, you can have students sample in both locations and compare and contrast the species collected.

There are many different methods that can be used to collect macroinvertebrates, as well as many different ways to sample their population. A dichotomous key should be used to identify the organisms. There is a plethora of dichotomous keys; for high school students the best option is a simple picture key because of the easy terminology. One for rivers can be accessed at *http://clean-water.uwex.edu/pubs/pdf/wav.riverkey.pdf* and one for ponds at *http://clean-water.uwex.edu/pubs/pdf/wav.pondkey.pdf*. Both of these keys were developed by the University of Wisconsin-Extension in cooperation with the Wisconsin Department of Natural Resources; the keys may be reproduced for educational purposes as long as proper credit is given.

Student Procedure

Collecting Insects in a Stream

1. Put the dip net onto the stream bottom, facing the net upstream.
2. For each pair of students, one person should stand in front of the net and gently kick the material on the streambed. Any insects present will flow downstream into the net.
3. Pick up any large rocks and gently brush any insects off into the net.
4. Dump the contents of the net into a shallow pan with some water.
5. Sort though the insects and use the key to identify them.
6. Record the data, including names and quantity of insects found, on a sheet of paper.

Collecting Insects in a Pond

1. Most of the insects in the pond will be on the edges near the vegetation. This is where the collecting should take place.
2. Insert the net into the water and sweep it just above the bottom, to avoid the mud, and then along the vegetation. Do a few sweeps.
3. Dump the contents of the net into a shallow pan with some water.
4. Sort through the insects and use the key to identify them.

5. Record the data, including names and quantity of insects found, on a sheet of paper

Optional Extension

If working in a stream, students could also conduct an index of biological integrity (IBI) study to determine the water quality of the stream. Visit the Save Our Streams Program website (*www.people.virginia.edu/~sos-iwla/Stream-Study/Methods/FormIntro.HTML*) to learn more about conducting an IBI and to obtain a data form. There are many different types of IBIs available online, but the Save Our Streams Program link is one of the easiest to use.

Once students are familiar with the aquatic macroinvertebrates, you could have the high school students team up with elementary school students to collect samples. Elementary students love working with older students, and it gives the older students a sense of accomplishment and pride to share what they know with younger students. Additionally, as every teacher knows, the best learning comes through teaching the material. At first, some high school students may be turned off by working with younger students, but we have found over several years that almost all of our high school students enjoy this experience. It is one item on the end-of-the-year class survey that the students say to keep doing.

Answers to Questions in Student Handout

1. The eight orders are Ephemeroptera (mayflies), Odonata (dragonflies and damselflies), Plecoptera (stoneflies), Hemiptera (true bugs), Megaloptera (dobsonflies), Coleoptera (beetles), Trichoptera (caddisflies), and Diptera (true flies, which include mosquitoes, midges, and black flies). The other groups are crustaceans, worms, and mollusks.
2. head, thorax, abdomen, six pair of legs, exoskeleton
3. piercing mouth part
4. mayflies, stoneflies, dragonflies, damselflies, dobsonflies
5. In complete metamorphosis the egg hatches into a larva, which then becomes a pupa. The larva and the pupa do not look like the adult. In incomplete metamorphosis the egg hatches into a nymph, which looks like the adult.
6. Answers will vary.

References

Singletary, E. (lead author), M. McGinley (contributing author), and L. A. Bledzki (topic editor). 2008. Common aquatic insects. In *Encyclopedia of Earth*, ed. C. J. Cleveland. Washington, DC: Environmental Information Coalition, National Council for Science and the Environment. *www.eoearth.org/article/Common_aquatic_insects*

University of Michigan Dearborn, Environmental Interpretive Center. n.d. Identifying aquatic insects. *www.umd.umich.edu/dept/na/aquatic_insecta/insect_metamorphosis.htm*

Aquatic Macroinvertebrate Identification

Student Handout

Background

Everyone is familiar with terrestrial insects such as dragonflies, houseflies, mosquitoes, and beetles, but many of us are unaware that many insects live in the water during their larval stages. These insects are part of a larger group of organisms called aquatic macroinvertebrates, which also includes crustaceans, worms, and mollusks. They are called macroinvertebrates because they can be seen with the naked eye and lack vertebrae. It is amazing what can be found in the water.

Objective

To identify common macroinvertebrates that live in streams and wetlands.

Materials Needed Per Pair of Students

- dip net (D-frame dip nets work best) for streams and wetlands or kick net for streams
- tweezers
- shallow pan
- dichotomous key for macroinvertebrates for streams and ponds
- dissecting scope
- informational note cards about insects

Procedure

Collecting Insects in a Stream

1. Put the dip net onto the stream bottom, facing the net upstream.
2. Have your partner stand in front of the net and gently kick the material on the streambed. Any insects present will flow downstream into the net.
3. Pick up any large rocks and gently brush any insects off into the net.
4. Dump the contents of the net into a shallow pan with some water.
5. Sort though the insects and use the key to identify them.
6. Record the data, including names and quantity of insects found, on a sheet of paper.

Collecting Insects in a Pond

1. Most of the insects in the pond will be on the edges near the vegetation. This is where the collecting should take place.
2. Insert the net into the water and sweep it just above the bottom, to avoid the mud, and then along the vegetation. Do a few sweeps.
3. Dump the contents of the net into a shallow pan with some water.
4. Sort though the insects and use the key to identify them.
5. Record the data, including names and quantity of insects found, on a sheet of paper.

Name________________________________

Questions on Aquatic Macroinvertebrates

1. List the eight orders of insects and the other groups of organisms that make up aquatic macroinvertebrates.

2. What features do all insects have in common?

3. What do true bugs have that other insects do not?

4. Which insects breathe through gills?

5. How are complete and incomplete metamorphosis different?

6. What macroinvertebrates did you collect the most of? The least of?

CHAPTER 11

Factors That Affect Eutrophication

Teacher Information

Background

Lakes, and waterways in general, can be classified into three types: oligotrophic, mesotrophic, and eutrophic. *Oligotrophic* refers to waterways with no excess nutrients and, therefore, no excess plant growth and a wide diversity of plant and animal life. Oligotrophic waterways typically are deep and clear, with colder temperatures; Lake Superior is a good example of an oligotrophic lake. The opposite of oligotrophic is *eutrophic.* A eutrophic waterway has an excess of nutrients, which results in an excess of plant growth and low biodiversity. Famous examples of eutrophic waterways include the Chesapeake Bay and the dead zone at the mouth of the Mississippi River in the Gulf of Mexico. Eutrophic lakes typically are shallow, have warmer temperatures, have mucky bottoms, and experience algal blooms. In the middle of these two extremes are *mesotrophic* waterways. Mesotrophic lakes contain some excess nutrients and plant growth.

Some areas of the world are so rich in nutrients as a result of human disturbance that they are classified as *hypereutrophic.* To give some scale, a typical eutrophic lake registers phosphates at >30 μg/L (parts per billion [ppb]); a hypereutrophic lake can have phosphate concentrations >100 μg/L. Eutrophication at these levels causes widespread algal blooms because of the excess of nutrients. These algal blooms significantly reduce the light that penetrates the water, killing many aquatic plant species. When the algae eventually die, they sink to the bottom of the lake and decompose. The decomposition process uses up dissolved oxygen from the water and turns it into gaseous carbon dioxide, effectively removing dissolved oxygen from the lake bottom. The lower oxygen levels can lead to regular fish kills.

Eutrophication is a natural process, though this process is usually accelerated by human interactions with the environment. It is estimated that 53% of lakes in the United States are eutrophic (International Lake Environment Committee (ILEC)/Lake Biwa Research Institute n.d.).

Eutrophication is usually due to an input of excess nutrients like nitrate and phosphate that are used to enhance agricultural output or to make residential lawns greener. It is usually phosphate that limits algae production in many lakes, but in some conditions nitrogen is the *limiting nutrient.* The limiting nutrient is a nutrient whose concentration in the environment of an organism determines the growth and productivity of that organism.

The main source of phosphates going into lakes is usually nonpoint pollution. Unlike *point source pollution*, which enters the water from specific locations (such as a regulated discharge pipe into the watershed), *nonpoint source pollution* comes from surface runoff from farms, lawns, septic systems, and anything dumped directly into the water or on the land in a surrounding watershed. One major source of nonpoint pollution in a rural watershed is past and present agricultural practices. Point source pollution in watersheds comes from companies that discharge water directly into the watershed, but the U.S. Environmental Protection Agency (EPA) regulates the amount of phosphate that can be discharged; therefore, companies and utilities usually do not make a big contribution of phosphate into watersheds today.

Objective

To investigate the effects of excess nutrients on algae.

Materials Needed Per Pair

- surface water sample (can be collected in advanced by one person, typically need 2–3 L per test)
- sunny window or plant grow lights
- deionized (DI) water (or any type of purified water)
- 14 200 ml beakers or plastic cups (Note: Since most commercial detergents contain phosphorus, try to thoroughly rinse glassware cleaned with soap before conducting any part of the experiment.)
- 7 plastic pipettes or droppers
- M potassium phosphate, dibasic solution (KH_2PO_4); this will be the phosphate pollutant
- M potassium nitrate solution (KNO_3); this will be the nitrate pollutant
- plastic wrap
- compound microscope (optional)
- slides and coverslips (optional)
- algae (optional)—any species will work
- Vernier sensors or water quality tests for turbidity and dissolved oxygen (optional)

Preparation of Solutions

- phosphate pollutant: 0.14 g of potassium phosphate (dibasic) to 100 ml of DI water

- nitrate pollutant: 0.10 g of potassium nitrate to 100 ml of DI water
- phosphate and nitrate pollutant: 0.14 g of potassium phosphate (dibasic) and 0.10 g of potassium nitrate to 100 ml of DI water

Suggested Class Preparation and Format

This investigation would be best used when studying water pollution and its effects on the environment. Although the investigation explores relatively mild contaminants, it could be useful when studying much more lethal contaminants like mercury or lead because it will demonstrate that it does matter what you put in the water, even in a small amount. There is also an important lesson to be demonstrated on the principle of "limiting reagents" in a chemical reaction (i.e., the reactants in a chemical reaction that limit the amount of product that can be formed). For aquatic plant life, there are three primary things that are required for algae to grow: sunlight, nitrogen nutrients, and phosphorus nutrients. Having ample access to all three will cause an algal explosion or bloom in the water. By restricting any one of these ingredients, algal growth will be limited. This investigation can provide a visual demonstration of this concept, which is central to all chemical reactions.

Preparing the phosphate and nitrate solutions along with setup for students will take a minimal amount of time. You can provide the surface water sample, ask the students to bring one, or start with DI water to which algae is added. If collecting a sample, it should be from stagnant water, such as a pond, within the top 0.5-1.0 m of water; plenty of algal cells should be found in the sample. If starting with DI water, algae can be purchased from a science supply company at minimal cost.

The dissolved oxygen test can be ordered from most science supply companies. Vernier has a relatively inexpensive turbidity meter that works well for this type of laboratory. If an electronic turbidity meter is not available, you can get stock commercial solutions of known turbidity from field test kit suppliers, and these stock solutions can be held next to the sample vial for comparison to determine approximate turbidity. If water quality tests of any sort are not available, the investigation can still be performed with visual measurements as represented in tables 11.1–11.5. To give students the option of having a "low" and "high" concentration of each of the pollutant solutions, just add 9 drops of pollutant to 100 ml of water to make a low concentration and 18 drops of pollutant to 100 ml of water to make a high concentration. The pollutants should be added to the water samples every day after data have been collected or whenever the students check the beakers. Use 100 ml water samples.

If labware is limited, the investigation could be divided among groups of students. One group could test only the effects of nitrate, while another could test only the effects of phosphate, and so on. In addition, plastic cups could be used in place of beakers. Student pairs could be assigned just one trial instead of two, and then class data could be combined.

Table 11.1. Pollutant Guide

Beaker	Amount of Nutrient
Control 1	None
Control 2	None
Low PO_4 1	9 drops of KPO_4
Low PO_4 2	9 drops of KPO_4
High PO_4 1	18 drops of KPO_4
High PO_4 2	18 drops of KPO_4
Low NO_3 1	9 drops of KNO_3
Low NO_3 2	9 drops of KNO_3
High NO_3 1	18 drops of KNO_3
High NO_3 2	18 drops of KNO_3
Low both 1	9 drops of KPO_4, 9 drops of KNO_3
Low both 2	9 drops of KPO_4, 9 drops of KNO_3
High both 1	18 drops of KPO_4, 18 drops of KNO_3
High both 2	18 drops of KPO_4, 18 drops of KNO_3

If the investigation is conducted in a traditional way (see Student Handout A), it will take one 50-minute class period for lab setup. The investigation will need to run for at least 10–14 days, so time will need to be set aside every other day or every three days for students to perform the water quality tests and to make observations. One 50-minute class period will be needed for data analysis. If the inquiry approach is used, an additional 50-minute period will be needed for students to conduct background research and design the investigation.

Methods

Collection of Surface Water

Rinse the collecting bottle out three times with sample water. Collect water from the top 0.5–1.0 m. Select a stagnant pond to ensure there will be algae present. Label the bottle with the location and refrigerate until used.

Testing the Effects of Nutrients on Eutrophication

1. Obtain 3 L of pond water from the teacher. [Teacher Note: As an alternative, students can collect their own samples.]
2. Measure the turbidity and dissolved oxygen content of the sample. Record the data on the table on your answer sheet.
3. Write down visual observations that include water color, clarity, and odor.

4. Pour 100 ml of pond water into a beaker. Repeat this step 13 more times, for a total of 14 beakers. Label the beakers as follows: control 1, control 2, low PO_4 1, low PO_4 2, high PO_4 1, high PO_4 2, low NO_3 1, low NO_3 2, high NO_3 1, high NO_3 2, low both 1, low both 2, high both 1, high both 2. [Teacher Note: This will give two trials for the investigation.]
5. Pollute the pond water samples with the appropriate amount of nutrients. Use Table 11.1 as a guide.
6. Cover the beakers with plastic wrap and set in a sunny window or under grow lights.
7. Check the beakers every 1–3 days. Perform steps 2–6 every time the beakers are checked. The only water quality tests that need to be performed regularly from now on are dissolved oxygen and turbidity.
8. Run the lab for 10–14 days. Beakers do not have to be checked on weekends.

Sample Data

The sample data shown here came from pond water already very high in phosphate; therefore, nitrate was the limiting factor. Most ponds will have more nitrate than phosphate, meaning that phosphate is the limiting nutrient.

Tables 11.2 and 11.3 show the observations for days 1 and 2.

Table 11.2. Observations on Day 1

Sample	Color	Clarity	Odor
Control 1	Clear	Good	None
Control 2	Clear	Good	None
Low PO_4 1	Clear	Good	None
Low PO_4 2	Clear	Good	None
High PO_4 1	Clear	Good	None
High PO_4 2	Clear	Good	None
Low NO_3 1	Clear	Good	None
Low NO_3 2	Clear	Good	None
High NO_3 1	Clear	Good	None
High NO_3 2	Clear	Good	None
Low both 1	Clear	Good	None
Low both 2	Clear	Good	None
High both 1	Clear	Good	None
High both 2	Clear	Good	None

Table 11.3. Observations on Day 2

Sample	Color	Clarity	Odor
Control 1	Clear	Good	None
Control 2	Clear	Good	None
Low PO_4 1	Clear	Good	None
Low PO_4 2	Clear	Good	None
High PO_4 1	Clear	Good	None
High PO_4 2	Clear	Good	None
Low NO_3 1	Clear	Good	None
Low NO_3 2	Clear	Good	None
High NO_3 1	Clear	Good	None
High NO_3 2	Clear	Good	None
Low both 1	Clear	Good	None
Low both 2	Clear	Good	None
High both 1	Clear	Good	None
High both 2	Clear	Good	None

After the first two days all beakers looked relatively the same—mostly clear water with no observed algal growth. However, by days 7 and 8 (Tables 11.4 and 11.5), all of the beakers with nitrate had more algal growth than the other beakers, which were still relatively clear.

Table 11.4. Observations on Day 7

Sample	Color	Clarity	Odor
Control 1	Clear	Good	None
Control 2	Clear	Good	None
Low PO_4 1	Green growth on bottom	Good	None
Low PO_4 2	Green growth on bottom	Good	None
High PO_4 1	Green growth on bottom	Good	None
High PO_4 2	Green growth on bottom	Good	None
Low NO_3 1	Green growth on bottom more than PO_4	Fair	None
Low NO_3 2	Green growth on bottom more than PO_4	Fair	None
High NO_3 1	Green on bottom, thicker with clumps of algae	Fair	None
High NO_3 2	Green on bottom, thicker with clumps of algae	Fair	None
Low both 1	Green growth on bottom more than PO_4	Fair	None
Low both 2	Green growth on bottom more than PO_4	Fair	None
High both 1	Green growth on bottom more than PO_4	Fair	None
High both 2	Green growth on bottom more than PO_4	Fair	None

SCILINKS
THE WORLD'S A CLICK AWAY

Topic: Eutrophication
Go to: *www.scilinks.org*
Code: WAT015

Table 11.5. Observations on Day 8

Sample	Color	Clarity	Odor
Control 1	Clear	Good	None
Control 2	Clear	Good	None
Low PO_4 1	Green growth on bottom	Good	None
Low PO_4 2	Green growth on bottom	Good	None
High PO_4 1	Green growth on bottom	Good	None
High PO_4 2	Green growth on bottom	Good	None
Low NO_3 1	Green growth on bottom more than PO_4	Poor	None
Low NO_3 2	Green growth on bottom more than PO_4	Poor	None
High NO_3 1	Green on bottom, thicker with clumps of algae	Poor	None
High NO_3 2	Green on bottom, thicker with clumps of algae	Poor	None
Low both 1	Thick green growth on bottom more	Poor	None
Low both 2	Thick green growth on bottom more	Poor	None
High both 1	Thick green growth on bottom	Poor	None
High both 2	Thick green growth on bottom	Poor	None

As you can see from Figure 11.1, dissolved oxygen levels are relatively the same until day 8, when the levels dropped in the beakers that experienced algae growth (beakers containing NO_3 pollutant). This is due to decomposition.

Figure 11.1 Dissolved Oxygen (DO) Levels

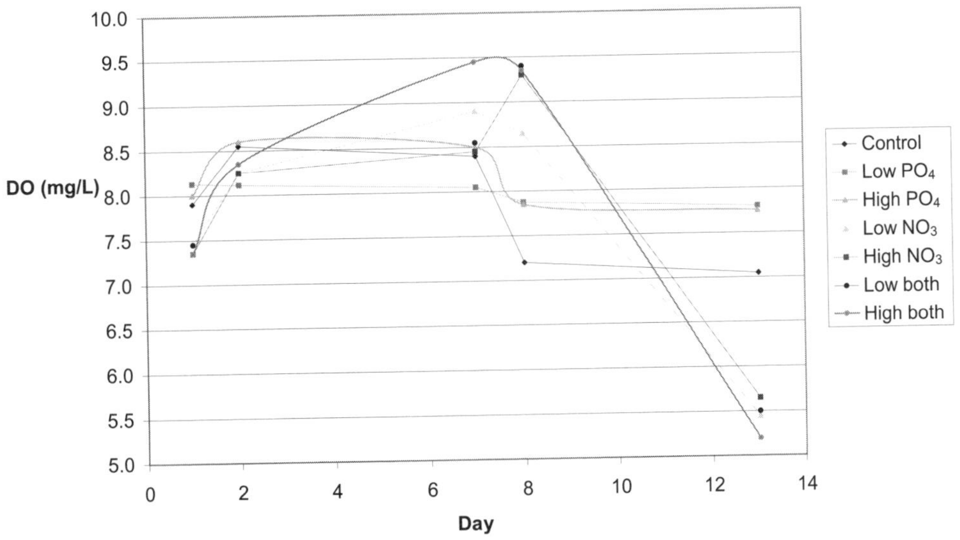

As shown on Figure 11.2, the turbidity of the samples containing nitrate was very high relative to the samples not containing nitrate. This is because the samples containing nitrate experienced the most algae growth.

Figure 11.2 Turbidity Levels (NTU = nephelometric turbidity unit)

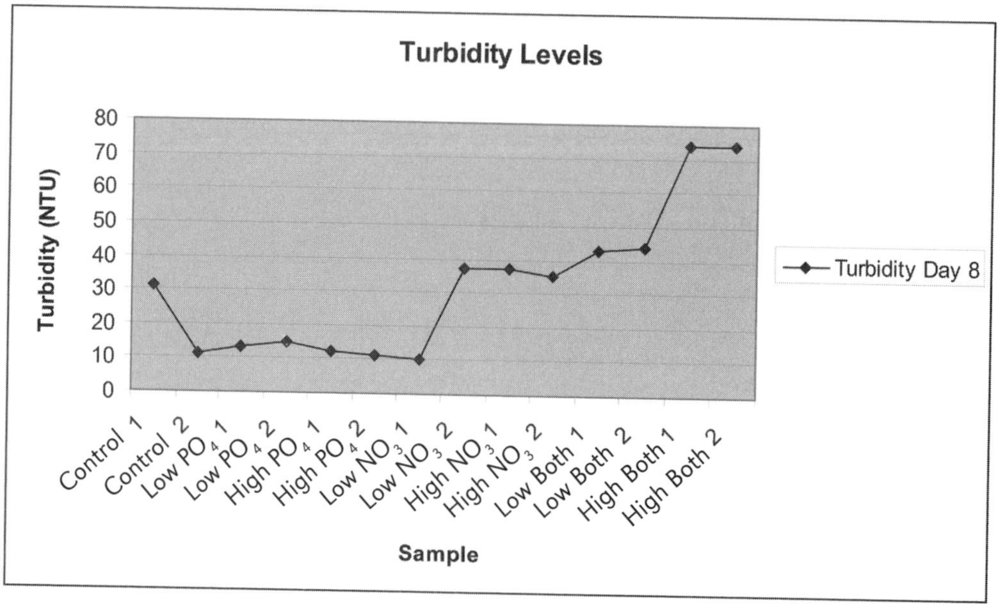

Optional Extensions

- If you do not have access to a turbidity meter, you can measure the amount of algae relative to the control by comparing the mass with an analytical balance. To find the mass of the algae, wait until the last day of the experiment and then filter the samples through preweighed filters and weigh the algae. Compare the mass of the experimental group with that of the control group to obtain a quantitative measure of growth.
- Sometimes in algal blooms there are a lot of blue-green algae because they can fix their own nitrogen. Other types of algae, which cannot fix their own nitrogen, have limited growth because of the lack of this nutrient. If you have diagrams available for students to identify the different types of algae, this would be an additional parameter to measure—to determine if types of algae concentrations change depending on availability of nutrients. Have the students examine samples of their pond water under the microscope and identify the algae present every time they check their beakers.

Answers to Questions in Student Handouts

1. PO_4
2. nonpoint sources, surface runoff
3. Answers will vary depending on starting water. Students should support their answer with data.
4. algal blooms on lake, mucky lake bottom, low oxygen levels on bottom of lake, fish kills
5. Homeowners can use low-phosphorus or no-phosphorus fertilizers on lawns. People living next to streams and waterways can leave a buffer strip. Farmers can use different farming methods to prevent soil erosion and buffer strips.

Reference

International Lake Environment Committee (ILEC) / Lake Biwa Research Institute, eds. n.d. *1988–1993 Survey of the state of the world's lakes.* 4 vols. Otsu, Japan: ILEC and United Nations Environment Programme (Nairobi).

Factors That Affect Eutrophication

Student Handout A

In this investigation, the effects of excess nutrients (nitrate and phosphate) on algae will be examined. An excess of these nutrients can lead to eutrophication in ponds and lakes. Eutrophic lakes typically are shallow, have mucky bottoms, and have warmer temperatures. These types of conditions lower the amount of oxygen available to aquatic organisms and sometimes can lead to fish kills. Usually eutrophic lakes are most noted for their algal blooms, which decrease the commercial and aesthetic value of the lake.

Objective

To investigate the effects of excess nutrients on algae.

Materials Needed Per Pair

- 2–3 L surface water sample
- sunny window or plant grow lights
- deionized (DI) water (or any type of purified water)
- 14 200 ml beakers or plastic cups
- 7 plastic pipettes or droppers
- phosphate solution (KPO_4)
- nitrate solution (KNO_3)

Methods

Collection of Surface Water

Rinse the collecting bottle out three times with sample water. Collect water from the top 0.5–1.0 m. Select a stagnant pond to ensure there will be algae present. Label the bottle with the location and refrigerate until used.

Testing the Effects of Nutrients on Eutrophication

1. Obtain 3 L of pond water from the teacher if not collecting it yourself.
2. Measure the turbidity and dissolved oxygen content of the sample. Record the data on the table on your answer sheet.
3. Write down visual observations that include water color, clarity, and odor.
4. Pour 100 ml of pond water into a beaker. Repeat this step 13 more times, for a total of 14 beakers. Label the beakers as follows: control 1, control 2, low PO_4 1, low PO_4 2, high PO_4 1, high PO_4 2, low NO_3 1, low NO_3 2, high NO_3 1, high NO_3 2, low both 1, low both 2, high both 1, high both 2.
5. Pollute the pond water samples with the appropriate amount of nutrients. Use Table 1 as a guide.

6. Cover the beakers with plastic wrap and set in a sunny window or under grow lights.
7. Check the beakers every 1–3 days. Perform steps 2–6 every time beakers are checked. The only water quality tests that need to be performed regularly from now on are dissolved oxygen and turbidity.
8. Run lab for 10–14 days. Beakers do not have to be checked on weekends.

Beaker	Amount of Nutrient
Control 1	None
Control 2	None
Low PO_4 1	9 drops of KPO_4
Low PO_4 2	9 drops of KPO_4
High PO_4 1	18 drops of KPO_4
High PO_4 2	18 drops of KPO_4
Low NO_3 1	9 drops of KNO_3
Low NO_3 2	9 drops of KNO_3
High NO_3 1	18 drops of KNO_3
High NO_3 2	18 drops of KNO_3
Low both 1	9 drops of KPO_4, 9 drops of KNO_3
Low both 2	9 drops of KPO_4, 9 drops of KNO_3
High both 1	18 drops of KPO_4, 18 drops of KNO_3
High both 2	18 drops of KPO_4, 18 drops of KNO_3

Name____________________________

Data Sheet and Questions About Eutrophication

Day___ Date _____

Sample	Color	Clarity	Odor	DO (mg/L)	Turbidity (NTU)
Control 1					
Control 2					
Low PO_4 1					
Low PO_4 2					
High PO_4 1					
High PO_4 2					
Low NO_3 1					
Low NO_3 2					
High NO_3 1					
High NO_3 2					
Low both 1					
Low both 2					
High both 1					
High both 2					

Note: DO = dissolved oxygen; NTU = nephelometric turbidity unit.

Make graphs of the dissolved oxygen and turbidity levels versus time and answer the following questions:

1. Which nutrient is the primary cause for eutrophication in a watershed?

____

____

____

2. From where does this nutrient mainly arise?

____

____

____

3. Which nutrient is the primary cause for eutrophication in your experiment? Explain how you know this.

____

____

____

4. What are some of the problems associated with excess nutrients?

____

____

____

5. What are some ways to prevent nonpoint source pollution?

____

____

____

Factors That Affect Eutrophication

Student Handout B

Objective

To investigate the effects of excess nutrients on algae.

In this investigation, the effects of excess nutrients (nitrate and phosphate) on algae will be examined. An excess of these nutrients can lead to eutrophication in ponds and lakes. Eutrophic lakes typically are shallow, have mucky bottoms, and have warmer temperatures. These types of conditions lower the amount of oxygen available to aquatic organisms and sometimes can lead to fish kills. Usually eutrophic lakes are most noted for their algal blooms, which decrease the commercial and aesthetic value of the lake.

The first step in designing this lab investigation is to define a hypothesis. An example of a hypothesis is as follows: *Phosphorus is a limiting nutrient for algal growth in our lake.* (Note that the type of surface water you collect will directly affect the outcome of this lab.)

State your hypothesis.

____

____

____

How will you test this hypothesis using the materials and methods listed in this handout? Think about the following questions:

1. What types of data should be collected to test the hypothesis?
2. What will you use as a control?
3. How many trials should there be?
4. How long should the experiment be carried out?
5. How will evaporation be reduced in your water samples?

Write down a step-by-step procedure, and create a data table for the results. Set up the experiment after the teacher has approved your procedure. When data collection is complete, enter it into a spreadsheet and into graph form and then answer the questions at the end of this handout.

Materials

- surface water sample (typically need 2–3 L/test)
- deionized (DI) water (or any type of purified water)
- sunny window or plant growth lights
- beakers
- plastic pipettes
- phosphate solution (KPO_4)
- nitrate solution (KNO_3)
- compound microscope (optional)
- slides and coverslips (optional)
- Vernier sensors or water quality tests for turbidity and dissolved oxygen (optional)

Method for Collection of Surface Water

Rinse the collecting bottle out three times with sample water. Collect water from the top 0.5–1.0 m. Select a stagnant pond to ensure there will be algae present. Label the bottle with the location and refrigerate until used.

Name________________________________

Questions About Eutrophication

1. Which nutrient is the primary cause for eutrophication in a watershed?

____

____

____

2. From where does this nutrient mainly arise?

____

____

____

3. Which nutrient is the primary cause for eutrophication in your experiment? Explain how you know this.

____

____

____

4. What are some of the problems associated with excess nutrients?

____

____

____

5. What are some ways to prevent nonpoint source pollution?

____

____

____

CHAPTER 12

Groundwater Contamination

Teacher Information

This investigation consists of two parts, in which students first model the effects of groundwater contamination and then track the flow of the contamination. However, Part I does not have to be done in order to do Part II. This Teacher Information section presents general information relevant to both parts of the investigation, followed by information specific to each part. There is a separate Student Handout for each part plus a question sheet (at the end of the chapter) covering both parts.

Background

Groundwater exists almost everywhere underground in between the spaces (pores) of the soil or gravel material. An *aquifer* is an underground layer of permeable material (e.g., rock, sand, or gravel). The area where the water fills the aquifer is called the *saturated zone*; above this zone, where there is no water, is the *unsaturated zone.* The division between these two zones is the *water table.*

A well must be drilled down past the water table into the saturated zone. As the well pumps up water, the water table drops and a *cone of depression* develops around the well; the surrounding water flows to the well. If there is too much demand and the water table is lowered enough, the well may go dry and a new well must be dug farther down into the water table. The water table may also be lowered during drought conditions. As groundwater is replenished from precipitation, eventually the water infiltrates the aquifer and then flows out to streams, lakes, ponds, or rivers.

Most people in the United States receive their drinking water from groundwater. In urban areas, the groundwater is treated and then passed on to the public. In rural areas, people use wells and have only the soil layers for water treatment. People living by a big surface water source such as the Great Lakes often have treated lake water. Surface water and groundwater are important resources that we must all take care of. Anything that is put on the ground can affect the water in the watershed either through surface runoff eventually to a lake or through infiltration of the soil and the groundwater. Either way you will eventually drink what you have put in the watershed.

In 1968, the Southwest Ottawa County Landfill (SWOCLF) was constructed in the vicinity of 168th Avenue and Riley Street in Holland, Michigan. At the time of its construction, the landfill was state of the art. The location of the landfill was on sandy soil, which is one of the best natural filters for water. Unfortunately, the groundwater had an average depth of only 15 ft. Sand is not only a good filter but also is porous and allows water to filter through quickly. The landfill received solvents, heavy metals, oils, sludges, municipal refuse, and drums containing unspecified contents, and these substances leached into the groundwater. Eventually, homes in the area had to be connected to city water because of the groundwater contamination. The landfill was closed in 1981.

Today the site has seven purge wells running constantly to pump out contaminated groundwater, which is run through a filtering process and then returns to the ground. The groundwater in that area flows directly toward Lake Michigan, near the location of the City of Holland's municipal water treatment intake pipe. Major concerns for contamination include benzene, trichloroethylene, ethyl ether, chlorobenzene, xylene, and iron. The site has been recapped with bentonite clay and designated a county park complete with trails, wetlands, and a sledding hill (U.S. Environmental Protection Agency [EPA] 2006).

Objectives

To (1) model the effects of groundwater contamination using an aquifer, sand, red dye, and a vacuum pump; and (2) to predict the flow of groundwater at the SWOCLF site with and without purging in order to track contamination.

Suggested Class Preparation and Format

This investigation would be best used when studying groundwater contamination. You can explain related groundwater terms ahead of time or show students the terms (e.g., *aquifer, saturated zone, unsaturated zone, water table,* and *cone of depression*) on the aquifer model.

The first part of this investigation, modeling groundwater contamination in an aquifer, will take one class period. The second part of the investigation, in which the students use real data from the SWOCLF and determine the flow of groundwater with and without purge wells for comparison, will take another class period, with remaining work assigned as homework. Note that Part I does not have to be done in order to do Part II.

The setup of this investigation is relatively simple. You could have one aquifer as a demonstration and record visual observations; or you could have students break into groups, with each group having its own aquifer, collecting samples of the water, and determining relative concentration of red dye on a colorimeter. To reduce mess, you may want to fill the aquifers with sand ahead of time.

Answers to Questions in Student Handout

1. Answers will vary.
2. Any well in a southwesterly direction from the SWOCLF to Lake Michigan.
3. Answers will vary.
4. The contaminants will be filtered out of the groundwater.
5. Answers will vary.
6. Answers will vary.

SCILINKS THE WORLD'S A CLICK AWAY
Topic: Contamination
Go to: *www.scilinks.org*
Code: WAT016

Contour Map 1 should have flow lines in a southwesterly direction from the SWOCLF to Lake Michigan. Contour Map 2 should show a flow line to the purge well and a cone of depression around MW-86.

Reference

U.S. Environmental Protection Agency (EPA). 2006. Southwest Ottawa County Landfill. *www.epa.gov/R5Super/npl/michigan/MID980608780.htm*

Groundwater Contamination
Part I: Modeling

Background

An *aquifer* is an underground layer of permeable material (e.g., rock, sand, or gravel). The area where the water fills the aquifer is called the *saturated zone*; above this zone, where there is no water, is the *unsaturated zone*. The division between these two zones is the *water table*.

A well must be drilled down past the water table into the saturated zone. As the well pumps up water, the water table drops and a *cone of depression* develops around the well; the surrounding water flows to the well. If there is too much demand and the water table is lowered enough, the well may go dry and a new well must be dug farther down into the water table. The water table may also be lowered during drought conditions. As groundwater is replenished from precipitation, eventually the water infiltrates the aquifer and then flows out to streams, lakes, ponds, or rivers.

Objective

To model the effects of groundwater contamination using an aquifer, sand, red dye, and a vacuum pump.

Materials Needed Per Group

- aquifer (see instructions below)
- coarse sand
- red dye
- vacuum pump
- colorimeter (optional)

Making an Aquifer

Making an aquifer to use as a model for groundwater flow is quite simple and can be very inexpensive. A 10 gallon fish aquarium or a Plexiglas model can be used. If using a fish tank, obtain a piece of glass to place inside the tank to divide it into two portions. Place the glass inside the tank so that one side has a width of approximately 10 cm. Use silicone caulk to secure the glass. This smaller compartment will act as your aquifer. Drill two holes into the side of the tank, one about 4 cm up from the bottom and one about 4 cm down from the top. Obtain tubing (clear is preferable), and insert the tubing into the holes and caulk. The top tube will be connected to a source of water such as the spigot on a faucet; the bottom tube will be the outflow of water from the aquifer and will need to drain into a sink or other container. You can purchase spigots that insert into tank, and then hoses could be connected to the spigots instead of being permanently attached to the tank.

If your school has a technology department, you may want to ask them to make a tank out of Plexiglas. In that case the tank could be constructed according to desired measurements. All joints of the tank should be caulked.

Refer to Figure 12.1 when making the aquifer.

Figure 12.1. Aquifer

Student Procedure

1. Fill the aquifer with coarse sand if not already done. As you fill the aquifer with sand, place a clear tube with a filter at the end of it about two-thirds of the way down in the middle of the aquifer, and continue to fill with sand. The top of the tube should be extended far enough out of the aquifer to be able to connect it with a vacuum apparatus.
2. Connect the top inflow tube to the aquifer and the water source. Fill the aquifer with water until all of the sand is saturated. Make sure the outflow tubing (bottom tube) is either clamped or held up above the tank. Shut off the water until step 4.
3. Using a plastic pipette, insert red dye into the aquifer. Place three squirts of red dye on either side of the vacuum pump tube at different depths.
4. Allow water to flow out of the aquifer, and at the same time turn the water back on at about the same rate as the outflow so the aquifer does not run dry or flood. Record your observations of dye movement on Data Table 1. Take notice of the dye that was placed at the top of the aquifer compared with dye that was placed at the bottom of the aquifer. Begin collecting water samples as the dye approaches the outflow. Collect water samples every 30 seconds. If using a colorimeter to determine the concentration of the dye, collect a cuvette full of water. If just making visual observations of the dye, use small

test tubes or glass vials to collect the water. Only a few milliliters of water are needed for the samples.

5. Allow the water to flow out until all the dye has been eluted.
6. Clamp the outflow tube and turn off the inflow. Insert the dye in the same way as you did in step 3.
7. Connect the vacuum tube to the vacuum apparatus. Simultaneously turn on the vacuum and the inflow and outflow of water. If your vacuum is very strong, turn up the inflow of water. Do not let your aquifer go dry—keep it saturated the whole time.
8. Record your observations of dye movement on Data Table 1. Take notice of the dye that was placed at the top of the aquifer compared with the dye placed at the bottom of the aquifer. Begin collecting water samples as the dye approaches the outflow. Collect water samples every 30 seconds. If available, use a colorimeter to obtain the concentration of the dye (record the concentration on Data Table 2).
9. Allow the water to flow out until all the dye has been eluted.
10. Turn off the inflow and continue to run the vacuum until the aquifer is dry.

Sample Data

Figure 12.2 show the relative concentration of dye with water samples collected every 30 seconds. The concentration goes up and down as the dye migrates through the aquifer. All of the dye migrates toward the bottom outflow tube.

Figure 12.2. Groundwater Contamination With Six Squirts of Red Dye

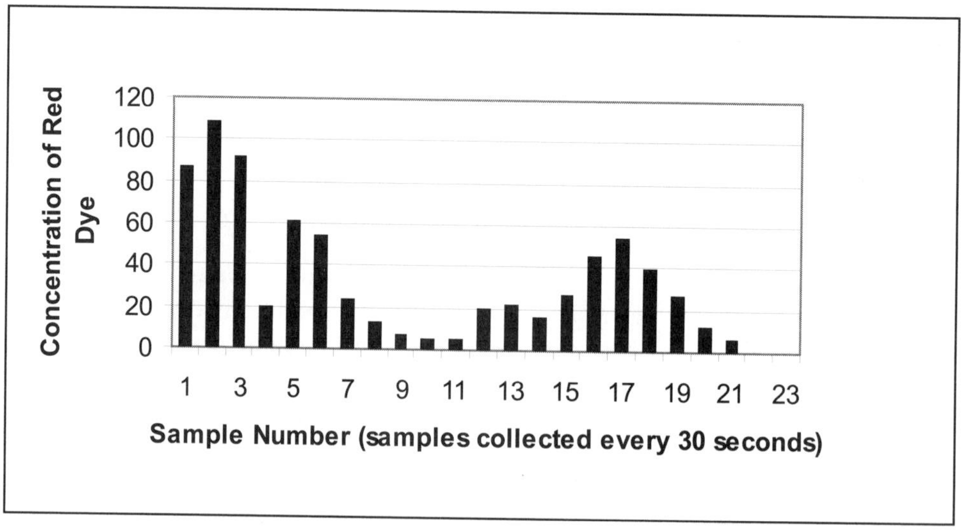

Figure 12.3 shows the water samples that were collected for Figure 12.2. As this photograph shows, it is not necessary to have a colorimeter to measure the concentration—students can see the difference in concentration as indicated by color.

Figure 12.3. Elution of Red Dye

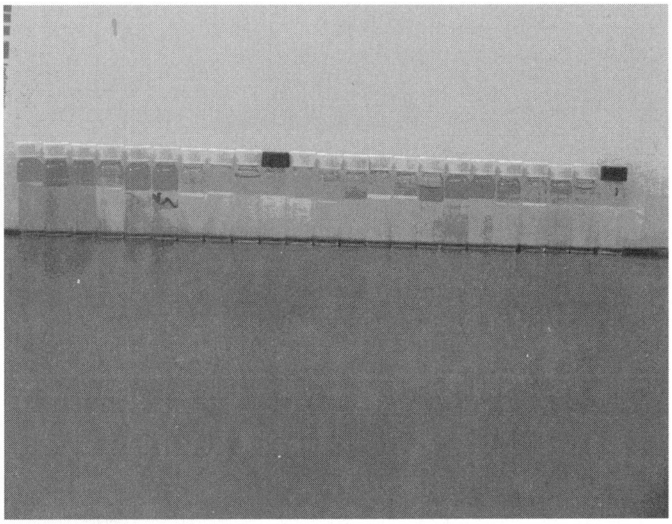

Figure 12.4 shows the relative concentration of red dye when the vacuum pump was turned on. Not as much dye was eluted because some was pumped out. The dye that was closest to the outflow tube and on the bottom of the aquifer was eluted. The dye that was closest to the outflow tube at the top of the aquifer was pumped out by the vacuum. The dye that is farthest from the outflow tube and upflow of the vacuum tube will always be pumped out by the vacuum, providing the vacuum is strong enough.

Figure 12.4. Groundwater Contamination With Purging

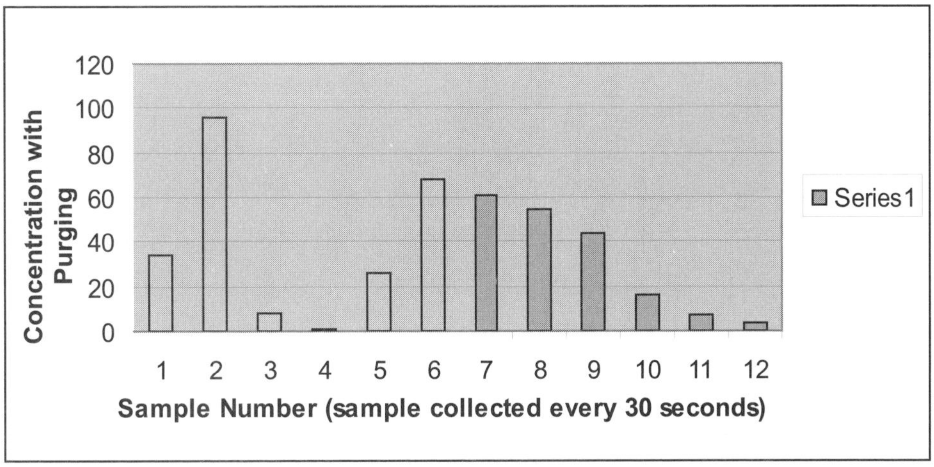

In Figure 12.5 the red dye is seen being eluted into outflow and taken up by the vacuum.

Figure 12.5. Red Dye With Vacuum

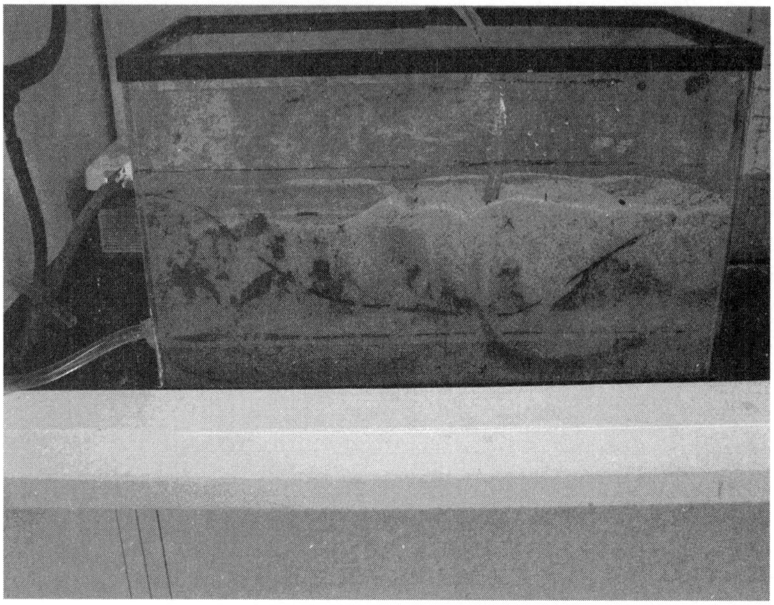

Optional Extensions

Possible variations of the variables in this investigation are unlimited. For example, you could change the coarseness of the sand used and then determine the effect it has on flow rate of the red dye. You could also change the locations and amount of red dye.

This part of the investigation could very easily be turned into an inquiry-based lab, with the students writing the procedure, as has been done with other investigations in this book.

SCILINKS THE WORLD'S A CLICK AWAY
Topic: Groundwater Contaminants
Go to: *www.scilinks.org*
Code: WAT017

Groundwater Contamination Part II: Tracking the Flow*

Background

The elevation of the water table can be depicted with contour lines, just like the elevation of land on a topographic map. The elevation of the water table is determined by the surface of wells, lakes, oceans, and groundwater-fed streams. The direction of the flow of groundwater can be identified by looking at a topographic map. Just as all rivers flow downhill or downslope, so does groundwater. Groundwater flow will be perpendicular to the contour lines and will always travel from an area of higher elevation to an area of lower elevation. The direction of groundwater is depicted with a line called a flow line. Numerous flow lines can be drawn as long as they do not cross each other.

When residents in the vicinity of the SWOCLF began to notice a weird smell like paint thinner after they turned on their faucets, being able to predict where the groundwater was flowing from was extremely important so that remedial action to clean up the contamination could be taken.

Objective

To predict the flow of groundwater at the SWOCLF site with and without purging in order to track contamination.

Materials

calculator

Student Procedure

1. Find the elevation of the water table in feet by subtracting the depth to the water table from the elevation of the well. Record all values on Table 1. [Teacher Note: Table 12.1 provides an answer key for Table 1.]
2. Transfer the elevations for the water table calculated in step 1 onto Contour Map 1 on the answer sheet.
3. Draw contour lines for the surface of the water table on Contour Map 1. Use a 1 ft. contour interval. Label the contour lines with the footages.
4. Draw a flow line from the SWOCLF to Lakeshore Ave. The flow line will not be a straight line and should be at right angles to the contour lines.
5. To eliminate the contaminants leaking into the groundwater from the SWOCLF, purge wells are put in to pump out the groundwater and filter it. If one purge well is located by MW-86, draw a new contour map show-

*Part II of this investigation was adapted from Geology Department lab at Western Michigan University.

ing the resulting cone of depression that will form around the well. Use the data in Table 12.2 with Contour Map 2. Use the scale on the map to find the distances from the purge well. If any wells are found to be within the given distances lower the water table elevation accordingly and write the new elevations down on Contour Map 2. Contour Map 2 should reflect the lowered water table levels from the purge well. Draw a new flow line from the SWOCLF to MW-86.

Reference

U.S. Environmental Protection Agency (EPA). 2006. Southwest Ottawa County Landfill. *www.epa.gov/R5Super/npl/michigan/MID980608780.htm*

Contour Map 1

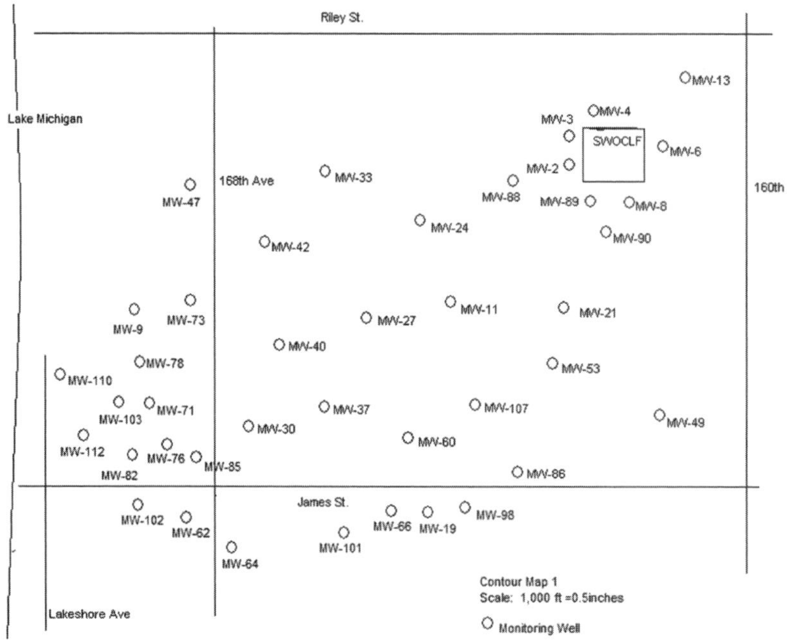

Contour Map 2

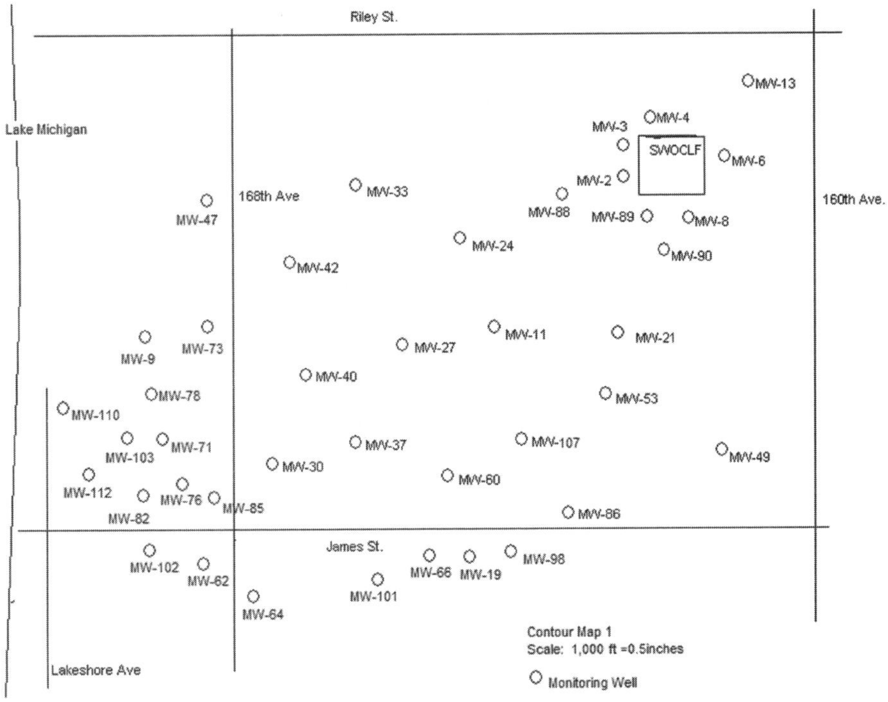

Table 12.1. Well Data

Well Number	Elevation of Well (ft.)	Elevation of Water Table (ft.)	Depth of Well (ft.)
MW-13	634	611	23
MW-6	618	610	8
MW-4	618	609	9
MW-8	620	608	12
MW-3	628	608	20
MW-2	614	607	7
MW-89	616	607	9
MW-90	614	607	7
MW-88	622	606	16
MW-21	618	606	12
MW-49	618	606	12
MW-86	612	606	6
MW-24	614	605	9
MW-11	612	605	7
MW-53	612	604	8
MW-107	612	603	9
MW-33	616	603	13
MW-98	610	603	7
MW-27	616	603	13
MW-19	616	602	14
MW-60	614	602	12
MW-42	618	602	16
MW-37	612	601	11
MW-66	614	601	13
MW-40	616	600	16
MW-101	610	599	11
MW-30	612	598	14
MW-47	614	598	16
MW-73	610	597	13
MW-64	610	597	13
MW-71	616	597	19
MW-85	612	597	15
MW-62	614	596	18
MW-78	614	595	19
MW-76	622	595	27
MW-9	612	594	18
MW-102	614	594	20
MW-82	614	593	21
MW-103	612	592	20
MW-112	622	591	31
MW-110	618	590	28

Table 12.2. Purge Well Data for Contour Map 2

Water Table After Purge Well	
Distance From Well (ft.)	**Water Table Lowered (ft.)**
500	20
1,000	15
1,500	10
2,000	5

Groundwater Contamination
Part I: Modeling

Student Handout

Background

An *aquifer* is an underground layer of permeable material (e.g., rock, sand, or gravel). The area where the water fills the aquifer is called the *saturated zone*; above this zone, where there is no water, is the *unsaturated zone.* The division between these two zones is the *water table.*

A well must be drilled down past the water table into the saturated zone. As the well pumps up water, a *cone of depression* develops around the well and the surrounding water flows to the well. If there is too much demand and the water table is lowered enough, the well may go dry and a new well must be dug farther down into the water table. The water table may also be lowered during drought conditions. As groundwater is recharged from precipitation, eventually the water infiltrates the aquifer and then out to streams, lakes, ponds, or rivers.

Objective

To model the effects of groundwater contamination using an aquifer, sand, red dye, and a vacuum pump.

Materials

- aquifer
- coarse sand
- red dye
- vacuum pump
- colorimeter (optional)

Procedure

1. Fill aquifer with coarse sand if not already done. As you fill the aquifer with sand, place a clear tube with a filter at the end of it about two-thirds of the way down in the middle of the aquifer, and continue to fill with sand. The top of the tube should be extended far enough out of the aquifer to be able to connect it with a vacuum apparatus.
2. Connect the top inflow tube to the aquifer and the water source. Fill the aquifer with water until all of the sand is saturated. Make sure the outflow tubing (bottom tube) is either clamped or held up above the tank. Shut off the water until step 4.

3. Using a plastic pipette, insert red dye into the aquifer. Place three squirts of red dye on either side of the vacuum pump tube at different depths.
4. Allow water to flow out of the aquifer, and at the same time turn the water back on at about the same rate as the outflow so the aquifer does not run dry or flood. Record your observations of dye movement on Data Table 1. Take notice of the dye that was placed at the top of the aquifer compared with the dye that was placed at the bottom of the aquifer. Begin collecting water samples as the dye approaches the outflow. Collect water samples every 30 seconds. If using a colorimeter to determine the concentration of the dye, collect a cuvette full of water. If just making visual observations of the dye, use small test tubes or glass vials to collect the water. Only a few milliliters of water are needed for the samples.
5. Allow the water to flow out until all the dye has been eluted.
6. Clamp the outflow tube and turn off the inflow. Insert the dye in the same way as you did in step 3.
7. Connect the vacuum tube to the vacuum apparatus. Simultaneously turn on the vacuum and the inflow and outflow of water. If your vacuum is very strong, turn up the inflow. Do not let your aquifer go dry—keep it saturated the whole time.
8. Record your observations of dye movement in Data Table 1. Take notice of the dye that was placed at the top of the aquifer compared with the dye placed at the bottom of the aquifer. Begin collecting water samples as the dye approaches the outflow. Collect water samples every 30 seconds. If available, use a colorimeter to obtain the concentration of the dye (record the concentration on Data Table 2).
9. Allow the water to flow out until all the dye has been eluted.
10. Turn off the inflow and continue to run the vacuum until the aquifer is dry

Name________________________________

Groundwater Contamination Modeling Data Sheet

Fill in Data Tables 1 and 2. When they are complete, make two line graphs for the aquifer with and without purging.

Data Table 1

Groundwater Flow		Groundwater Flow With Purging	
Observations of Dye Movement		Observations of Dye Movement	
Top of Aquifer	Bottom of Aquifer	Top of Aquifer	Bottom of Aquifer

Data Table 2

Groundwater Flow		Groundwater Flow With Purging	
Time	Concentration of Dye	Time	Concentration of Dye

Groundwater Contamination Part II: Tracking the Flow

Student Handout

Background

In 1968, the Southwest Ottawa County Landfill (SWOCLF) was constructed in the vicinity of 168th Avenue and Riley in Holland, Michigan. At the time of its construction, the landfill was state of the art. The location of the landfill was on sandy soil, which is one of the best natural filters for water. Unfortunately, the groundwater had an average depth of only 15 ft. Sand is not only a good filter but also is porous and allows water to filter through quickly. The landfill received solvents, heavy metals, oils, sludges, municipal refuse, and drums containing unspecified contents, and these substances leached into the groundwater. Eventually, homes in the area had to be connected to city water because of the groundwater contamination. The landfill was closed in 1981.

Today the site has seven purge wells running constantly to pump out contaminated groundwater, which is run through a filtering process and then returns to the ground. The groundwater in that area flows directly toward Lake Michigan, near the location of the City of Holland's municipal water treatment intake pipe. Major concerns for contamination include benzene, trichloroethylene, ethyl ether, chlorobenzene, xylene, and iron.

The elevation of the water table can be depicted with contour lines, just like the elevation of land on a topographic map. The elevation of the water table is determined by the surface of wells, lakes, oceans, and groundwater-fed streams. The direction of the flow of groundwater can be identified by looking at a topographic map. Just as all rivers flow downhill or downslope, so does groundwater. Groundwater flow will be perpendicular to the contour lines and will always travel from an area of higher elevation to an area of lower elevation. The direction of groundwater is depicted with a line called a flow line. Numerous flow lines can be drawn as long as they do not cross each other.

Objective

To predict the flow of groundwater at the SWOCLF site with and without purging in order to track contamination.

Materials

calculator

Procedure

1. Find the elevation of the water table in feet by subtracting the depth to the water table from the elevation of the well. Record all values on Table 1.
2. Transfer the elevations for the water table calculated in step 1 onto Contour Map 1 on the answer sheet.
3. Draw contour lines for the surface of the water table on Contour Map 1. Use a 1 ft. contour interval. Label the contour lines with the footages.
4. Draw a flow line from the SWOCLF to Lakeshore Ave. The flow line will not be a straight line and should be at right angles to the contour lines.
5. To eliminate the contaminants leaking into the groundwater from the SWOCLF, purge wells are put in to pump out the groundwater and filter it. If one purge well is located by MW-86, draw a new contour map showing the resulting cone of depression that will form around the well. Use the data in Table 2 with Contour Map 2. Use the scale on the map to find the distances from the purge well. If any wells are found to be within the given distances lower the water table elevation accordingly and write the new elevations down on Contour Map 2. Contour Map 2 should reflect the lowered water table levels from the purge well. Draw a new flow line from the SWOCLF to MW-86.

Name______________________________

Groundwater Contamination Parts I and II Questions

Part I Question:

1. Describe the differences in the flow of groundwater between the tanks when water was not pumped out with a vacuum and when it was pumped out.

____

____

____

Part II Questions:

2. Based on Contour Map 1, which water well(s) is/are most likely to become contaminated?

____

____

____

3. If the groundwater is flowing at a rate of 4 ft./day, how long will it take the contaminants from the landfill to reach the lake? (Use the formula *Time* = *Distance/Velocity*). Give your answer in years.

____

____

____

4. What effect will the new purge well have on the contaminants originating from the landfill?

____

____

____

5. How is the vacuum you used in Part I similar to the purge well you learned about in Part II?

____

____

____

6. Do you think the purge wells are able to filter all of the contaminants from the groundwater?

____

____

____

Attach the completed table and contour maps.

Table 1. Well Data

Well Number	Elevation of Well (ft.)	Elevation of Water Table (ft.)	Depth of Well (ft.)
MW-13	634		23
MW-6	618		8
MW-4	618		9
MW-8	620		12
MW-3	628		20
MW-2	614		7
MW-89	616		9
MW-90	614		7
MW-88	622		16
MW-21	618		12
MW-49	618		12
MW-86	612		6
MW-24	614		9
MW-11	612		7
MW-53	612		8
MW-107	612		9
MW-33	616		13
MW-98	610		7
MW-27	616		13
MW-19	616		14
MW-60	614		12
MW-42	618		16
MW-37	612		11
MW-66	614		13
MW-40	616		16
MW-101	610		11
MW-30	612		14
MW-47	614		16
MW-73	610		13
MW-64	610		13
MW-71	616		19
MW-85	612		15
MW-62	614		18
MW-78	614		19
MW-76	622		27
MW-9	612		18
MW-102	614		20
MW-82	614		21
MW-103	612		20
MW-112	622		31
MW-110	618		28

Contour Map 1

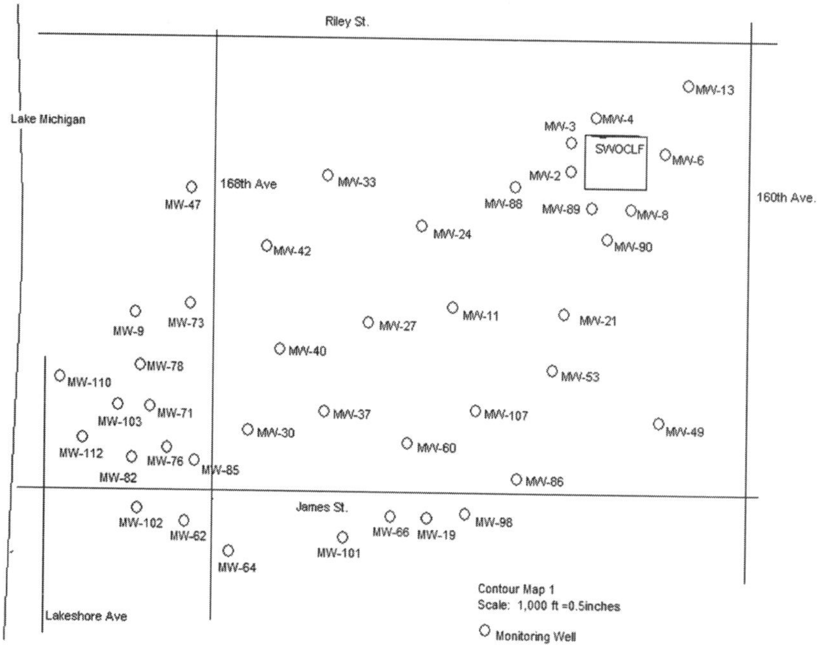

Table 2. Purge Well Data for Contour Map 2

Water Table After Purge Well	
Distance From Well (ft.)	**Water Table Lowered (ft.)**
500	20
1,000	15
1,500	10
2,000	5

Contour Map 2

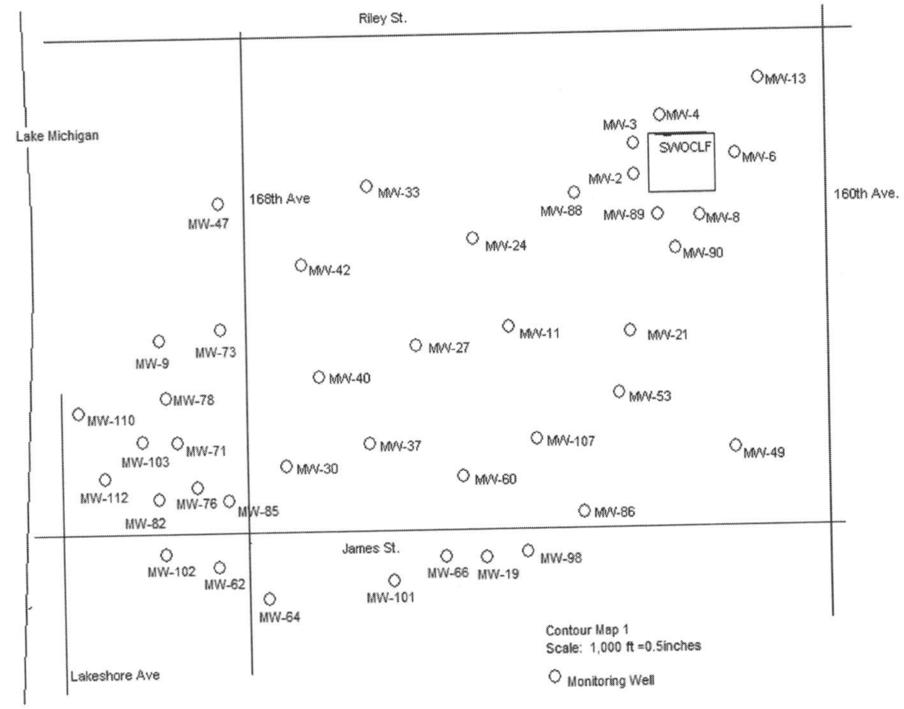

APPENDIX

A

The Macatawa Watershed, Holland, Micigan

Freshwater may be our most essential resource on Earth and the most important nutrient to our bodies. Water makes up 70%–75% of our body weight, and we use water in every bodily function (Gilliam n.d.). In fact, if we did not have access to clean water we would die. Fortunately for those who live in Michigan, access to clean water has not been a problem; the Great Lakes contain about 20% of all the freshwater on earth (U.S. Geological Survey [USGS] 2008). However, there is one little lake with a tiny watershed that has received attention from the U.S. Environmental Protection Agency (EPA) because it is rich in nutrients and drains right into Lake Michigan. The investigations in this book analyze how geology (Chapters 1 and 2), settlement (Chapters 3–8, 10, and 12), and agriculture (Chapters 9 and 11) have all contributed to the hypereutrophic status of Lake Macatawa.

A watershed is the land area where all the water drains into a bigger body of water such as a stream, river, or lake. Watersheds are based on topography and land area. The Macatawa watershed refers to all the land area that drains water to Lake Macatawa. There are 179 square miles that transport water into Lake Macatawa, either directly or into a hydrologically connected tributary.

Everyone lives in several watersheds, because each stream, river, pond, and lake has its own watershed area. In this location, there is the Great Lakes drainage basin (a drainage basin is a watershed on a much bigger scale), the Macatawa watershed, the Macatawa River watershed, and smaller watersheds for each stream and tributary.

The Macatawa watershed is nearly circular, with half of it in the southwestern part of Ottawa County and half of it in the northwestern part of Allegan County. The watershed includes two main cities, Holland and Zeeland, and many small villages, but approximately 70% of its land use is agricultural (Michigan Department of Environmental Quality n.d.).

Lake Macatawa is really nothing more than a drowned river mouth, like many of the lakes along the coast of Lake Michigan. The lake itself has a long, slender shape and has two bays on the north side, Big Bay and Pine Creek Bay. The lake is approximately 4.5 mi. long; it is 870 ft. wide at its narrowest point and 6,035 ft. at its widest. It has an average depth of 12 ft., and its deepest point is 38 ft. The main river in the watershed is the Macatawa River, which flows into Lake Macatawa. There are several other small streams that flow directly into the lake, such as Pine Creek and Kelly Lake Drain. There are three major tributaries flowing into the Macatawa River: Noordeloos Creek, the North Branch of the Macatawa River, and the South Branch of the Macatawa River.

A hypereutrophic lake is a lake that is very high in nutrients. To give some scale, a typical eutrophic lake registers phosphates at >30 μg/L (parts per billion [ppb]); a hypereutrophic lake can register phosphates at >100 μg/L. Eutrophication at these levels causes widespread algal blooms because of the excess of nutrients. When the algae eventually die, they sink to the bottom of the lake and decompose. The decomposition process uses up dissolved oxygen from the water and turns it into gaseous carbon dioxide, effectively removing dissolved oxygen from the lake bottom. The lower oxygen levels can lead to regular fish kills. Lake Macatawa regularly has phosphate levels around 200 μg/L.

Learning about Lake Macatawa and its watershed will help everyone understand their own watersheds. Understanding watersheds is important because, in addition to depending on water for survival, many people use water for recreational activities such as boating, fishing, and swimming. Seeing how humans can negatively impact the environment through the investigations in this book will help us learn how to choose land management strategies that have positive effects on the watersheds in which we live.

More information about the Macatawa watershed is available at the Macatawa Area Coordinating Council website, *www.the-macc.org*.

References

Gilliam, M. n.d. Water: The body's most important nutrient. *Sissel-Online Article Resource* (Health and Fitness News Article 12). *www.sissel-online.com/article/water.php*

U.S. Geological Survey (USGS). 2008. *The water cycle: Freshwater storage. http://ga.water.usgs.gov/edu/watercyclefreshstorage.html*

Michigan Department of Environmental Quality (MDEQ). n.d. *A hydrologic study of the Macatawa River watershed.* MDEQ, Land and Water Management Division, Water Management Section, Hydrologic Studies Unit. *www.michigan.gov/documents/deq-water-mgmt-macatawa_4698_7.pdf*

APPENDIX B

Lab Report Rubric

The report must be typed in 12 pt. font with 1 in. margins. Paragraphs and complete sentences are a must.

Parts of the Lab Report

Please include the following items in the following order, with the italicized words used as headings in your paper.

- ☐ *Title Page:* This page contains the title of the lab experiment, author names, institution name, class name, and date.

- ☐ *Abstract:* The abstract should be written last. This is a brief summary of the main points of your lab report.

- ☐ *Introduction:* This section includes a discussion of background information relating to the experiment. You should also provide a description of the problem, a statement of the hypothesis, and identification of the variables and the control.

- ☐ *Materials and Method:* This section presents the procedure for the lab. State how the problem was tested and the materials used in enough detail so that another person could replicate the experiment. The procedure must be written in paragraph form and must *not* contain pronouns (I, she, her, him, he, they, we, it, etc.) or words like "next," "then," or "finally." Always name what is being talked about.

- ☐ *Results:* Describe observations and discuss data in written form. Data must also be displayed in table and graph forms. Make sure tables and graphs are titled and labeled appropriately.

- ☐ *Conclusion:* Discuss what the data mean (e.g., do they show trends, is the relationship positive or negative), whether it proved or disproved your hypothesis, and what could be done better or what further testing could look like. Draw conclusions from the data.

Scoring

50–47 points: Lab report follows directions, supplying an abundance of information in each category. No grammatical errors. Uses a technical writing style.

46–45 points: Lab report follows directions, supplying a minimum amount of information in each category. No more than two grammatical errors.

44–42 points: Lab report follows directions, with an effort made to adequately cover the information requested in each category. Few grammatical errors.

41–40 points: Lab report follows directions but is lacking in quantity and/or quality of information.

39–35 points: Lab report does not follow directions very well and lacks in quality and quantity of information.

34–30 points: Lab report does not follow directions, and information is inaccurate.

Index

Page numbers in **boldface** refer to figures.